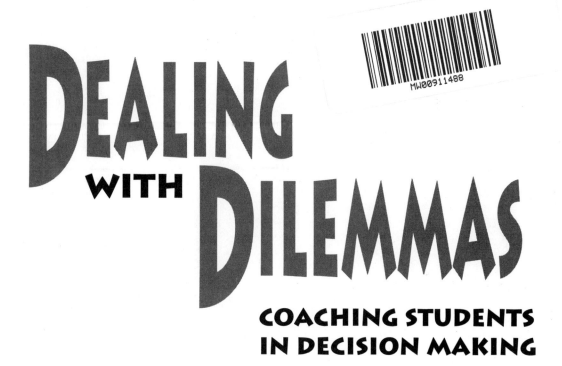

DEALING WITH DILEMMAS

COACHING STUDENTS IN DECISION MAKING

D. Mark Meyers
Assistant Professor of Education
Rowan University

J. Doyle Casteel
Professor Emeritus of Education
University of Florida

Good Year Books
A Division of Addison-Wesley Educational Publishers, Inc.

Good Year Books

are available for most basic curriculum subjects plus many enrichment areas. For more
Good Year Books, contact your local bookseller or educational dealer. For a complete
catalog with information about other Good Year Books, please write:

Good Year Books
1900 East Lake Avenue
Glenview, IL 60025

Book design: Jess Schaal
Managing Editor: Bobbie Dempsey
Production/Manufacturing Director: Janet Yearian
Senior Production Coordinator: Fiona Santoianni

0-673-36369-4

1 2 3 4 5 6 7 8 9 - ML - 06 05 04 03 02 01 00 99 98

This Book Is Printed
On Recycled Paper

FOR OUR CHILDREN

CONTENTS

INTRODUCTION: SOME OBJECTIVES, DEFINITIONS, ASSUMPTIONS, AND A SPORTING PROPOSITION

Students are faced with decision-making situations every day. Often, these situations require them to deal with dilemmas. The dilemmas can be creations of students or their social surroundings. Helping students acquire and practice the use of decision-making skills so that they can deal with a given dilemma is and should be a basic goal of instruction in grades four, five, six, seven, and eight. The central purpose of *Dealing with Dilemmas* is to present teachers and teacher trainees with an approach to meeting this goal. The approach allows students to practice decision-making skills in a variety of contexts in school. It presumes that those who teach English, science, social studies, and other classes will teach decision making along with the academic ideas, concepts, and themes they present in class. The cross-context use of the decision-making skills gives students the opportunity to practice the skills in a variety of situations, increasing the likelihood that they will use the decision-making skills when they encounter dilemmas in their daily lives.

Specific Objectives

Dealing with Dilemmas is a how-to-do-it book. Six specific objectives have influenced the way this book is organized:

1. To describe and present examples of five different types of structured dilemmas that teachers may use to help students acquire and practice decision-making skills.

2. To present materials that teachers may use to assess the practicality of the different types of structured dilemmas described and presented.

3. To provide structured dilemmas related to three social processes that tend to be present in any group—including

groups within the classroom—the processes of conflict, cooperation, and competition.

4. To provide decision-making exercises related to two social conditions that students are likely to encounter with some frequency—power and relative deprivation.

5. To delineate one approach that teachers may use to employ each type of decision-making exercise presented.

6. To identify and sequence the steps used to develop original structured dilemmas of different types.

Decision-Making Skills

Among the skills applicable in dealing with structured dilemmas through decision making are policy skill, consequential skill, outcome skill, criterial skill, and emotive skill.[1] These five skills are defined in terms of learning conditions and anticipated student responses in Figures 1–5. For each of the five skills, the learning conditions needed to elicit desired student behavior are listed to the left, and the initial student behavior sought within these learning conditions is listed to the right. If the behavior listed to the right occurs in response to the conditions on the left, then the skill identified is said to be displayed by the student.[2]

Figure 1. **Policy Skill Defined in Terms of Learning Conditions and Critical Student Response Behavior**

Learning Conditions to Be Established

1. Presentation of a social situation in which an individual or group needs to make a decision.

2. Provision of a policy that is relevant to the social situation presented.

3. Two or three policies, none of which are relevant to the social situation presented.

4. Directions to the effect that students are free to identify the one policy that is relevant to the social situation presented.

Student Response Behavior

Students will identify with the one policy that is relevant to the given social situation.

Example:
As a demonstration of policy skill, students will be able to demonstrate their understanding of a social situation by identifying policies which are relevant to a given social situation. For example, the decision to bomb Hiroshima was the product of policies relevant to the social situation. Students need to establish relevance for any policies and decisions they use as a part of a decision-making exercise. The ability to establish relevance is a vital tool for student understanding. Without it, decision making will be flawed.

Copyright © 1999 Good Year Books.

[1] Generic learning skills such as listening, observing, reading, recording, and communicating are, of course, important aspects of decision making. The intent here, however, is to define different acts of valuation and decision making with some precision and from the perspective of the classroom.

[2] These definitions were first published in a slightly different form in J. Doyle Casteel and Miriam Williford, *Planning Cross-Cultural Lessons*, 1975. A National Seminar Publication of the Latin American Studies Association.

Figure 2. Consequential Skill Defined in Terms of Learning Conditions and Critical Student Response Behavior

Learning Conditions to Be Established

1. A social situation in which an individual or group has been required to make a decision is presented.

2. The decision made by the individual or group in the social situation is identified and described.

3. One set of three or four results, i.e., consequences, likely to eventuate from the decision made in the given situation, is provided.

4. Two or three other sets of results, unlikely to eventuate from the decision made in the given situation are provided.

5. Directions to the effect that students are to identify the one set of results likely to occur as a result of the decision made in the given social situation.

Student Response Behavior

Students will select the one set of consequences most likely to result from the decision made in the social situation presented.

Example:

As a demonstration of consequential skill, students will be able to demonstrate their understanding of the consequences for one's decisions. If their forced-choice format, for example, students will be placed in the position of making a decision from a given set of consequences. In order to distinguish between the options presented, students will need to identify the consequence of each decision.

Figure 3. Outcome Skill Defined in Terms of Learning Conditions and Critical Student Response Behavior

Learning Conditions to Be Established

1. An end or outcome that an individual or group wishes to achieve is identified. (This end is easy to visualize, e.g, to own a bicycle, be chosen as a cheerleader, or to win a prize in a contest.)

2. A social situation providing a context within which the outcome desired is to be sought by an individual or group is presented.

3. One policy relevant to the social situation presented and likely to enable the person or group to attain in the desired outcome is provided.

4. Two or three policies, all relevant to the social situation presented but unlikely to yield the desired outcome, are provided.

5. Directions to the effect that students are to identify the one policy likely to yield the desired outcome.

Student Response Behavior

Students will select the one policy that is likely to yield the desired outcome within the context of the given social situation.

Example:

In the dilemma "The Laws of the Boppers" the outcome established by the leader is clear, laws that everyone can understand. By practicing outcome skill, the students' decisions take this outcome into account.

Figure 4.   Criterial Skill Defined in Terms of Learning Conditions and Critical Student Response Behavior

**Learning Conditions
to Be Established**

1. A criterion that is to be applied in order to make a decision is presented and explained. (The criteria is relatively abstract, e.g., fairness, justice, loyalty, reciprocity.)

2. A social situation in which a decision is to be made is presented.

3. One policy, germane to the given social situation and consistent with the standard of judgments that is to be applied, is provided.

4. Two or three policies, relevant to the given social situation but consistent with the standard of judgment that is to be applied, are presented.

5. Directions to the effect that students are to identify the one policy that is consistent with the given criterion.

**Student
Response Behavior**

Students will select the one policy that is consistent with the criterion that has been given as the standard of judgment to be applied in the social situation presented.

Example:

In the dilemma "A Ship in Trouble," as a captain of the ship, students must establish a criterion upon which they will make their decision. Criterial skill will enable the teacher, and student, to identify whether their decisions fulfill criterion.

Figure 5.   Emotive Skill Defined in Terms of Learning Conditions and Critical Student Response Behavior

**Learning Conditions
to Be Established**

1. An emotional state is identified and explained, e.g., love desire, jealousy, envy, or rage.

2. A social situation in which an individual or group needs to make a decision is presented.

3. One option, likely to be adopted by an individual who is experiencing the given emotional state, is provided.

4. Two or three options, relevant to the given social situation but unlikely to be adopted by a person who is experiencing the given emotional state, are provided.

5. Directions to the effect that students are select the one policy more likely to be adopted by an individual who is experiencing the given emotional state.

**Student
Response Behavior**

Students will select the one policy likely to be opted for by an individual experiencing the given emotional stage within the context of the social situation given.

Example:

In the dilemma "As Others See Us," students are presented with an opportunity to use emotive skill by identifying the policies which would most likely be selected by a person experiencing the emotional situation of discrimination.

Structured Dilemmas

One of the means by which you may help students acquire and refine decision-making skills is to select or write structured dilemmas relevant to the content being taught. Structured dilemmas create learning conditions in which students, working in small groups, are likely to exhibit two or more of the five skills defined in Figures 1–5.

Structured dilemmas written in five formats will be presented in subsequent chapters. Each chapter will consist of five sections, in the following order:

1. *Functions* of the format of the structured dilemma.
2. A *Description* of the components that are used to build the type of structured dilemma presented in each chapter.
3. *Classroom Examples* of the format developed in each chapter.
4. *From the Teacher's Perspective*, one approach that teachers might employ to use examples of each format.
5. *On Your Own*, a presentation of step-by-step directions that teachers might follow to develop their own examples of each format. A detailed example is presented in Chapter 6.

Some Assumptions

Several assumptions are made with regard to structured dilemmas. Some of them are presented here, not to convince so much as to forewarn.

1. *Decision making is tied to understanding. If an issue or a situation is comprehended poorly, the decisions made are unlikely to be wise no matter how adequately decision-making skills are applied.* Each of the structured dilemmas presented in subsequent chapters is focused on a social situation in the guise of a short story. Students must comprehend the situations if the decision sheets are to work as intended.

2. *Instructional materials are not intended to teach. Rather, they are instruments to be used by teachers.* It is the teacher who selects or writes a structured dilemma for student use; who provides directions that help students perceive purpose in what they are doing; who monitors student behavior and maintains a learning climate; who organizes students into learning groups; and who provides feedback on student performance. In common with other instructional resources, structured dilemmas are a tool for teaching, not a substitute. Although each chapter contains a section in which one approach is delineated, this section should be as a suggestion, not as a prescription.

3. *To function most effectively, instructional materials must be made relevant to two worlds of experience.* The child lives in a world of experience in which certain events and situations appear important. Instructional materials should focus on the child's world and draw on the student's interest. At the same time, there are societal events and situations that may be referred to as the adult's world of experience. Structured dilemmas used to exemplify the types of dilemmas in the chapters that follow are intended to present significant adult concerns in terms of events and situations that belong to the child's world of experience.

4. *Relevant decision-making situations can provide students with opportunities to practice conflict resolution skills.* Children are confronted with dilemmas that place them in conflict with their peers, older students, or adults. Students are expected to practice conflict resolution in such situations. However, students are often placed into these situations without preparation. While it is impossible to provide practice for every possible situation students may encounter, structured dilemmas provide students with a means to practice conflict-resolution skills. It is important to note that the practice of conflict-resolution skills in these exercises do not end with the social situations. Additionally, teachers can lead student groups to practice conflict-resolution skills when groups are attempting to form a consensus and when comparing the ideas of different groups through metacognition.

5. *Decision making and the study of organized bodies of knowledge, such as science, history, or literature, may be and ought to be coordinated.* What one learns in science may be made applicable to such topics as the quality of our environment or the energy crisis by placing students in decision-making situations in which they have an opportunity to display and use their knowledge and understanding. Using such knowledge in decision-making situations that are made relevant to the students' world of experience provides these students with an opportunity to perceive that such knowledge and understanding have personal and social utility. The students experience the answer to the age-old question, "What good will this do me when I grow up?" Structured dilemmas that appear in subsequent chapters are related to personal and social dimensions of five concepts: cooperation, conflict, competition, power, and relative deprivation. Teachers who write their own structured dilemmas may relate them to concepts they are teaching, topics they are exploring, themes they are examining, issues they are analyzing, or ideas and principles they are

DEALING WITH DILEMMAS

asking students to validate. History students can use the structured dilemma format to practice decision-making skills in social situations that present the issues and concepts faced by leaders of the time. Students would be able to see the difficulties faced by the leaders.

6. *The classroom teacher should not hesitate to create and maintain structures that are likely to eventuate in desired student learnings.* It is sometimes argued that if teachers talked less and students talked more, students would learn more and have more interest in school. It is also asserted that if teachers ask good questions, then teaching success is likely to follow. Neither of these contentions is totally valid. While teachers may structure so frequently as to inhibit or bar student behavior, they are responsible for creating learning conditions, including constraints, within which it is believed students will learn. While teachers frequently employ questions to solicit desired student behaviors, they do so within a structured learning situation. The assumption that teachers should structure learning conditions is most obvious in the sections entitled "From the Teacher's Perspective" in subsequent chapters. There, importance is placed on providing learning set, learning closure, and how to give careful directions.

7. *Decision-making skills are learned, maintained, and rejected or modified in groups.* For this reason, the structured dilemmas provided in Chapters 2–5 contain at least two decision sheets. The first decision sheet is to be used by students individually in order to react personally to a social situation. The second decision sheet is to be used by students in organized groups of four to five members. Hence, if initial and individual reactions differ, these differences must be resolved in order to complete the group decision sheet, providing practice for conflict-resolution skills. Stated another way, the group decision sheet triggers decision-making behavior, as discussed above, because initial reactions to situations become an aspect of the exercise and are subjected to scrutiny, criticism, and use of the group.

A Sporting Proposition

Prior to studying subsequent chapters, you are invited to test the utility of the approach presented. To determine whether the use of structured dilemmas with small groups of students will result in student use of decision-making skills, take the following steps:

1. Choose one of the structured dilemmas presented in Chapter 2.

2. Make five or six copies of the structured dilemma.

3. Secure a tape recorder or video camera.

4. Select a group of four or five students. Ask them to study the social situation at the focus of the structured dilemma you selected. (Do not distribute the decision sheets yet.)

5. Ascertain that students have understood the social situation.

6. Ask students to complete the individual decision sheet.

7. Start recording.

8. Explain that students are to share individual reactions and then to seek consensus. (You may need to explain what it means to seek consensus.)

9. Have students work together in order to complete the group decision sheet.

10. Dismiss the students, and rewind the tape.

11. View (listen) to the tape in order to answer these questions:

    Did students use *policy* skill?
    > (Can the students identify policies relevant to the social situation?)

    Did students use *consequential* skill?
    > (Can students identify the consequences generated by their decisions?)

    Did students use *outcome* skill?
    > (Can students identify a policy that will yield a desired outcome?)

    Did students use *criterial* skill?
    > (Can students establish and use a criterion that is consistent with a given situation?)

    Did students use *emotive* skill?
    > (Can students identify the policy most likely to be chosen given an emotional state?)

12. Determine the degree to which the structured dilemma worked for you.

13. Now that you have observed for yourself how structured dilemmas elicit the use of skills from decision-making groups, you are ready to move on to the following chapters.

1

THE STANDARD FORMAT OF STRUCTURED DILEMMA

· ·

Functions

The standard format of structured dilemma emphasizes that there is a personal form of knowing and understanding. Although knowledge and understanding are acquired in numerous ways, the processes of information acquisition and processing may be clarified by referring to three levels of reading for knowledge and understanding.

A poem, novel, newspaper article, or book may be read in order to comprehend what the author has to say within the context in which she chose to communicate with her reader. The objective in this case is to comprehend, and the first level is referred to as the *comprehension* level of learning.

A poem, novel, newspaper article, or book may be read in order to enhance the understanding of an issue, idea, topic, theme, or concept. In this case, one must understand what the author expressed in her context. But the elements of the author's message that are relevant to the issue must also be identified and attended to—the idea, topic, theme, or concept that should be understood better as a result of reading. The objective in this case is, at the least, to analyze; and such analysis may lead to synthesis and evaluation. Together, they are referred to as the *analytical* level of information acquisition and processing.

A poem, novel, newspaper article, or book may also be read in order to clarify a personal position with regard to social issues and situations. In this case, the author's message must first be understood in context. Such understanding tends to be enhanced if the author's message is analyzed. The primary objective, however, is to objectify a person's beliefs with regard to social issues and situations. The objective here is to gain insight into beliefs and commitments—or the *personal* level of learning.

The standard format of structured dilemma is intended to elicit these three types of behavior from students: comprehension, analysis, and personalization of information and ideas. These behaviors can allow students to acquire and practice conflict-resolution skills. The standard format of structured dilemma provides teachers with a means to assist students in developing persuasive skills and confronting moral choices and questions in the classroom environment. The connection between the academic material being studied and the students' own lives provides a means for teachers to tap into their own lives for learning situations rather than relying exclusively on situations created in a textbook.

Description

The standard format of structured dilemma contains four components: (1) a social situation; (2) comprehension directions and questions; (3) relational directions and questions; and (4) value/feeling directions and questions.

The social situation may be created in a variety of ways. Select a section from a play, novel, or short story that is relevant to the topic, concept, or idea that you are teaching; select a cartoon, picture, graph, or table of statistical data that is relevant to the topic, concept, or idea that you are teaching; or select a current events article from a magazine or newspaper that is relevant to the current focus of class study. Recordings of songs or speeches can also be used to establish a social situation. Develop an instructional resource and use this to establish a stimulus situation. You may choose to write social situations that reflect the behavior and concerns of the class.

The social situation, regardless of its source or form, should meet three criteria. First, it must be relevant to the class in which it is to be used. Consequently, a source might be useful in a history class but not relevant to a biology class. Second, the selected resource should match the current educational development of the class, which can vary in each group of students. The resource must be one from which students can acquire information and frame interpretation in relation to the content they are studying at the time structured dilemma is used. Third, the resource must be one that deals with an event, situation, or set of behaviors toward which students can form preferences and express personal reactions. Hence, the resource must be from a context with which the students are familiar, either from their own experiences or from previous class materials.

The second component of the standard format of structured dilemma consists of five or six comprehension discussion starters. Discussion starters are directions or questions to which students may respond in order to study the social situation and acquire information. Some conventions according to which comprehension discussion starters may be written are

Who was present?

Who was involved?

Who acted first?

When did this event occur?

When did he leave?

When did he become upset?

Describe the hallway where the fight occurred.

List the places that she went.

Where did the action occur?

Where was she going?

What was her goal?

What did John do?

Describe the object Lisa found.

How long did it take the man to act?

For how long did the woman believe this?

How much money was involved?

How much time was spent?

How many people were present?

How many days did it take?

These conventions may be summarized: ask questions beginning with the words *who, when, where, what, how long, how much,* and *how many* that can be answered by referring to the stimulus situation that students are provided.

Other conventions according to which comprehension discussion starters may be phrased are

Quote a line or two from the stimulus situation; ask students to express the meaning of the quotation in their own words.

Focus attention on a paragraph or an element of a picture or song; ask students questions—who, when, where, what, how long, how much, and how many.

Quote a selection from the stimulus situation; cite a word or phrase used in the source; ask students to define the word or term using the context provided in the situation.

Define a word or phrase used in the stimulus situation; ask students to volunteer illustrations consistent with the definition you gave.

The third component of a standard format of structured dilemma consists of two to four relational discussion starters. These are questions or directions that enable students to frame relationships between the information and knowledge presented in the stimulus situation and the topic, theme, concept, or idea they are currently studying. In effect, students use relational discussion starters to search for elements that may be made relevant to what they are currently studying in the class where the standard format of structured dilemma is used.

Some conventions according to which relational discussion starters may be written are

Define the concept at the focus of study; ask students to find an example of the concept in the social situation.

Define the concept at the focus of study; cite an instance of behavior in the social situation; ask students to explain why the behavior is an example of the concept.

Cite the theme you are teaching, e.g., fear; ask students how the theme is reflected in the social situation.

Cite the theme you are teaching; review with students how this theme was presented in a resource previously studied; review with students how the theme is presented in the current social situation; ask students how the two presentations differ, or ask students how the two presentations are similar.

Cite the theme you are teaching; cite an element of the social situation; ask students how the element cited presents an aspect of the theme being studied.

Suggest a number of themes you have taught; cite an instance of behavior in the social situation; ask students to identify the theme that is depicted by the instance cited.

Cite the idea you are teaching; cite data presented in the social situation; ask students how the data support the idea.

Cite the idea you are teaching; cite data presented in the social situation; ask students how the data might be used to question the validity of the idea being taught.

Ask students to state the idea at the focus of study; ask students to identify elements of the social situation that support the idea, or ask students to identify elements of the social situation that might be used to question the validity of the idea.

Ask students to identify the idea at the focus of study; point out an idea that is presented in the social situation; ask students how the two ideas differ or are similar.

Ask students to define the concept at the focus of study; point out an instance of behavior in the social situation; ask students to explain why the instance of behavior is an example of the concept.

Define, or ask students to define, the concept at the focus of study; point out an instance of behavior in the social situation; ask students if the instance is an example of the concept at the focus of study. After students have responded, wait, saying nothing so that they may volunteer statements about how they reasoned; if they fail to do so, be prepared to use probing questions to secure an explanation.

Define, or ask students to define, the concept at the focus of study; cite an instance of behavior presented in the social situation; ask students to explain why the behavior cited is not an example of the concept.

Cite the topic you are teaching; ask students to identify aspects of the social situation that are relevant to the topic.

Identify the topic that is the current focus of study; point out an aspect of the social situation; ask students why the aspect is relevant.

Ask students to identify the topic that is at the focus of study; point out one aspect of the social situation; ask students how the aspect is relevant to the current topic of study.

Identify the topic that is the focus of study; designate one aspect of the social situation; ask students to explain why the aspect is not relevant to the topic of study.

Similar conventions may be used if a standard format of structured dilemma stresses an issue that is being analyzed or if a principle that is being validated by students is assigned. The function of these conventions is to help students frame relationships between the social situation used to construct the standard format of structured dilemma and the concept, topic, theme, idea, or issue that is currently being studied by students.

The fourth and final component of a standard format of structured dilemma consists of value/feeling discussion starters. Value/feeling discussion starters are questions and directions that encourage students to react to the stimulus situation by expressing personal preferences; considering what might be or what should be done in the situation; exploring the consequences of events or possible options that might be exercised; identifying criteria that might be used to justify different courses of action; or sharing personal feelings.

Some of the conventions you may employ to write value/feeling discussion starters are presented here. Some of them are likely to result in one- or two-word responses. In such cases, wait to see if students explain or clarify their answers. If students fail to elaborate, ask them to provide explanations or clarifications. This use of "wait-time" needs to become habitual for both teachers and students in order to allow students to complete their answers. Conventions according to which value/feeling discussion starters may be written are

Cite or describe a social condition; ask students if the condition is good.

Cite or describe a social condition; ask students if the condition is bad.

Cite or describe two or more social conditions; ask students which condition is best.

Cite or describe two or more social conditions; ask students which condition is worst.

Cite or describe a social problem; place a student within this problem situation; ask the student what might be done to resolve the problem.

Cite or describe a social condition; ask a student to imagine that she is involved; ask the student what she would do.

Cite or describe a social situation; cite or describe a procedure that might be used in this situation; ask students to identify possible consequences.

Describe an emotional state; describe a social situation; ask students how the emotional state might influence behavior in the situation given.

Cite or describe an emotional state; cite or describe a social situation; place a student within this condition; ask the student if the emotional state is good, or ask the student if the emotional state is bad.

Describe a social problem; cite a policy that has been selected; place the student within this condition; ask the student to demonstrate that the policy adopted is reasonable, or ask the student to demonstrate that the policy is unreasonable.

Value/feeling discussion starters written according to these conventions are intended to allow students to personalize their understanding of standard types of resources that are typically used in the classroom; hence the name, standard format of structured dilemma. The standard format is the backbone of structured dilemmas. The decision-making strategies utilized in the other formats later in the book are based on the students' ability to understand the situations presented.

Classroom Examples

Ten examples of the standard format of structured dilemma are provided here. Study at least four of them, paying particular attention to the student behaviors most likely to be elicited by the discussion starters. This approach should enable you to understand the sections dealing with the use and construction of standard format examples of structured dilemma. You may also use the examples of the standard format to practice writing other formats of structured dilemmas. The social situation has been developed already; the decision-making situations will need to be created utilizing the methods presented in the chapter that are appropriate to the format desired.

TOM'S DUTY

Social Situation

Tom Franklin is a very good football player. As a linebacker, he has helped his club team win six games. They have lost only once, and one game remains to be played.

This Saturday, Tom's team will play another good team. The other team has also won six games and also has one tie on its record. If Tom's team wins they will be the champions of the conference. If they lose, then the other team will be champions.

Tom is looking forward to the game. He is a loyal member of his team.

Tom is also a school leader. Tom wants his school to be one of the best schools. Last week, the principal asked him to serve on a committee.

The principal said, "Tom, it is time we took a look at the school handbook we use to introduce new students to our school. We need students like you to revise it."

Tom was pleased that he was asked to serve on the committee. He quickly agreed to do what the principal asked.

He said, "I would like to be on the committee. When will we meet?"

The principal answered, "The first and most important meeting is next Monday, right after school. It is very important that all committee members be present for that meeting."

"I'll be there," Tom said.

On Friday, it rained all day. Early Saturday morning, Tom's football coach called him.

The coach said, "Tom, we are not playing today. The field is flooded. We'll play for the championship on Monday afternoon, right after school is dismissed. See you then."

After hanging up the phone, Tom thought, "Oh, no, I forgot. I promised the principal I would attend a committee meeting on Monday night."

Tom called his school principal. The principal said, "It's too bad that both the game and the meeting are scheduled for the same time. It's too late to change the meeting. I'm afraid you'll have to choose which event is more important to you."

Tom answered, "I feel bad about this. But, I'm going to play in the football game."

Even as he spoke, Tom was unhappy. One part of him wanted to play in the game, and the other wanted to attend the committee meeting.

Discussion Starters

COMPREHENSION

1. What game does Tom play?

2. How good is Tom's team?

3. How many games has the other team won?

4. When is Tom's team supposed to play?

5. Why is the game delayed?

6. Tom agrees to become a member of the school committee. What is the purpose of the committee?

RELATIONAL

7. Tom decides to play in the game. How does this conflict with what the principal expected?

8. Suppose Tom had decided to attend the meeting. How might this have caused conflict with the other members of his team?

9. Tom wants to be loyal to his team. Tom wants to be loyal to his school. How are his two desires in conflict?

VALUE/FEELING

10. Tom decided to play in the football game. Was this a good decision?

11. If you had been Tom, what would you have done?

12. If you had made the decision Tom made, how would you have felt?

DEALING WITH DILEMMAS

Kathy's Ambition

Social Situation

Kathy is ambitious. She wants to be an excellent student. She wants to learn to play the piano well. She is a member of numerous clubs, both in school and out of school.

Kathy is also talented. She can be an excellent student. She can, with practice, play the piano well. She is a leader in a number of clubs.

All her life, Kathy has made one mistake over and over. She tries to do too many things at once, which prevents her from doing any of them as well as she might.

Take this afternoon, for example. To prepare for school tomorrow, Kathy must finish a book report for English, study for a science test, and complete her geography assignment. She is also supposed to go for a piano lesson and attend two different club meetings.

Not knowing what to do, Kathy told her mother she was ill and went to bed.

Discussion Starters

COMPREHENSION

1. Kathy wants to do three things. Name them.

2. What school assignments is Kathy supposed to finish this evening?

3. Besides preparing for school, what else does Kathy need to do today?

4. What bad mistake does Kathy often make?

5. What does Kathy decide to do?

RELATIONAL

6. This afternoon, Kathy's desire to be a good student is in conflict with her desire to play the piano well. Why?

7. Suppose Kathy also wants to be honest with her mother. To what extent is Kathy's statement that she is ill in conflict with her desire to be honest?

8. Kathy wants to be good at everything she does. Kathy tries to do more than she should attempt. How is her behavior in conflict with her desire?

VALUE/FEELING

9. Kathy went to bed rather than try to do all the things she could not hope to get done. What would you have done?

10. Suppose you were Kathy. If you were, what would you do to avoid this problem in the future?

11. If you were Kathy, how would you explain your failure to have your work done when you attend school tomorrow?

Bouncers, Fly Balls, Butterfingers, and Victories

Social Situation

At Robinson Elementary School, it was a hot day. It was already hot in Mrs. Geegan's classroom when the school day began. By 11:00 A.M. students were so hot they could hardly listen to Mrs. Geegan. It was hard to pay attention. By early afternoon, it was almost impossible to breathe in the room.

Mrs. Geegan said, "We've got to get out of here. I'll tell you what. Let's go outside and play softball."

Some of Mrs. Geegan's students liked this idea. They said, "You're a great teacher, Mrs. Geegan."

Other students, however, did not like the idea. They shared their feelings.

"It's too hot to play softball."

"It's too dirty out there."

"The gnats and flies will eat us alive."

"You've got to be kidding."

Mrs. Geegan responded, "Whatever we do, we will have to do it together."

Bob, one of the students, said, "Why don't we all go outside? It's much cooler out there. Those who want to play softball can play. Those who don't want to play can talk with each other and watch the game."

Everyone agreed with Bob's idea. Soon, twenty of Mrs. Geegan's students had chosen teams and were playing.

For the first two innings, everyone was happy. Then in the top of the third inning, things began to go wrong.

The first batter in the inning hit a high bouncing ground ball toward second base. Tony, who was playing at second base, knew it was a sure out. But, he took his eyes off the ball. The ball hit the tip of his glove and bounced into the outfield. The runner was safe.

Cindy yelled at Tony, "Butterfingers!"

Greg said, "Who told you that you knew how to play?"

Linda got into the act: "Which team are you playing for? Ours or theirs?"

The next batter hit a soft fly ball in the direction of Susan in the outfield. Susan lost the ball in the sun. She could not catch the ball. This put runners on second and third.

Tony was the first to speak. "Girls should not be allowed to play this game. They've all got butterfingers. They can't catch. They can't hit. They can't run. The only thing they know how to do is lose."

Cindy answered Tony, "Look who's talking!"

Soon, most of the boys and girls on the teams were shouting at one another. Mrs. Geegan blew her whistle. Gradually, the boys and girls became quiet.

Mrs. Geegan asked the members of the teams in the field to form a small circle around her. When the twenty boys and girls were ready, Mrs. Geegan said:

"To have fun when you play a team sport, you must cooperate; to win you must cooperate; to play any team game well, all

members of a team must support all other members."

She continued, "If we cannot play the game correctly, we will have to go back inside. I do not want to go back, and I don't think you want to go back into that hot room either. When a member of your team makes a mistake, that person needs your support. If a team member does well, he or she can support themselves. Do you understand?

"Yes, Mrs. Geegan," was the response from the twenty team members.

Members of the two teams continued to play for about another hour. Tony had a lot of chances at ground balls; he did not make another error. Susan also played well.

When the game was over, the other team was ahead by a score of 13 to 11.

"They won," Susan said.

"But it was close," Tony added.

Hearing Tony and Susan talk, Mrs. Geegan said, "Your team won something too."

Discussion Starters
COMPREHENSION

1. Why does Mrs. Geegan want to leave her classroom?

2. When Mrs. Geegan suggests playing a game, some of her students disagree. Why don't they want to play?

3. How is the argument over going outside settled?

4. After the game started, there was an argument. What caused the argument?

RELATIONAL

5. When people work together to secure a common goal, they cooperate. Mrs. Geegan says that all team sports require cooperation. Do you agree?

6. Mrs. Geegan also insists that her class cooperate before students are allowed to go outside. Name some ways in which class members can cooperate.

VALUE/FEELING

7. Mrs. Geegan says it is good to help people when they make a mistake. Would you help a teammate who made a mistake that cost your team a game?

8. Suppose you wanted to help a person who made a mistake that cost your team a big game. How might you help the person who made the mistake?

9. Let's say you are one of the girls who chose not to play. When Susan fails to catch the ball, Tony says girls should not be allowed to play. When Tony says this, how do you feel?

10. Mrs. Geegan said, "We'll play as a team, or we'll all go inside." Was this a good way to handle the problem?

When Two Oxen Are Stuck in the Mud

Social Situation

Once upon a time, there was a planet called Luxor. On the planet of Luxor, there was a land called Luxland.

The people of Luxland were a simple, happy group of people. Most of them lived in villages located in the valleys of the vast mountains. Most Luxlanders earned their living by farming. In each village, there were craftspeople who made shoes, ox harnesses, and tools that the farmers used. Most of the time the farmers traded what they grew for the things the village craftspeople made.

The Luxlanders who lived in villages seldom used money. Sometimes they had a few pieces of gold or silver. Since they had no money, Luxlanders did not ask a craftsperson how much a cart for hauling crops would cost in money. Instead, Luxlanders asked, "How many bushels of grain will you accept in exchange for this cart?"

Each year, the villagers of Luxland sent some of the grain they had grown to the one city in Luxland, Lux City. All the farmers of a village got together and chose one man to go to the city. He kept a careful record of how much grain each farmer gave him to take to the market. He kept a careful record of what each person wanted from the city. To be chosen to make this trip was a great honor and a great responsibility.

One year when the crops were good, Ulford was selected by his village to go to the city. He loaded his cart and set off to the city. Normally, it would take him three days to reach the city. Ulford knew it would be a longer trip that year. The rains had been heavy. In the mountains that he must cross, many of the roads would be damaged. Also, the crops had been especially good that year, so Ulford was carrying more grain than was usually taken to the city. All of this would slow him down.

By the third day, Ulford was a little more than halfway to Lux City. He came to a place where three village roads met. About the time that Ulford reached this junction, carts from two other villages also arrived. Like Ulford's cart, these too were heavily loaded.

"Crops have been good in all villages this year," Ulford thought. "Grain will be plentiful in Lux City. Those who want grain will bargain hard. Perhaps I can beat the other carts to Lux City."

About five miles later, the main road to Lux City ran next to a stream. Although the road was open, Ulford could tell the road had recently been under water.

Ulford started across the flat area that had been flooded. Soon his cart was mired in mud almost up to the axle. Ulford climbed down from his cart and tried to help his oxen. Even with his help, the oxen could not move the cart. Ulford did not know what to do. Looking over his shoulder, he saw that the other carts had stopped when

DEALING WITH DILEMMAS

· ·

they saw that he was stuck.

Ulford waded through the mud back to the other carts. He said, "We'll never get through to Lux City."

The driver of one of the other carts said, "If we work together, we can all get across this bad spot. First we'll use all six oxen to move your cart. Then we'll use all six to move the second cart. And finally, we'll use all six oxen to move my cart."

"That sounds great," Ulford said.

Using the six oxen, the three men moved their carts past the part of the road that had been flooded. Two days later, all three carts arrived at Lux City, one after the other. It was obvious to everyone that the three men driving the three teams of oxen were good friends who enjoyed one another's company.

Discussion Starters

COMPREHENSION

1. Describe the land of Luxland.

2. How do the people of Luxland earn a living?

3. When a Luxlander wants to buy something, what does he use instead of money?

4. Who is Ulford?

5. How is Ulford honored by the people of his village?

6. How does Ulford make friends with two men from villages other than his own?

RELATIONAL

7. When people work together to get something they all want, they cooperate. The village craftspeople and the farmers cooperate to earn a living. How?

8. When people share resources, such as oxen, to succeed in doing something they all want to do, they cooperate. How do the three men cooperate in order to reach Lux City?

9. When people cooperate with one another, they are likely to trust and like one another. Which parts of the story support this idea?

VALUE/FEELING

10. When Ulford first saw the two other villagers, he wanted to get to the city before they did. He hoped this would make his load of grain more valuable. Was this a good attitude?

11. Each year one man is chosen to go to Lux City. If you were helping to make the choice for your village, what type of person would you select?

12. Study your response to question 11. Explain your answer.

No Prize for Second Place

CONCEPTUAL FOCUS: COMPETITION

Social Situation

A school carnival was recently held at Robertsville Middle School. The purpose of the carnival was to raise money for the school. The teachers at Robertsville want to start a new reading program. They need new books, new videos, and new computers with software.

At first, many of the teachers and most of the students were not very interested. Mr. Cotter, the principal, thought, "I must do something to create interest in the carnival. Otherwise, we will not make enough money to start a new reading program."

After thinking about what he might do, Mr. Cotter made an announcement:

"The sixth-grade homeroom that makes the most money may have a pizza party. The school will furnish the pizzas and the sodas.

"The seventh-grade homeroom that makes the most money will be given free tickets to a college football game. The school will pay for the bus that will transport students to and from the game. The university has agreed to give us end-zone tickets.

"The eighth-grade homeroom that makes the most money will be given free tickets to see a movie at one of the local theaters. Mr. Drake, who owns the theaters, has given Robertsville tickets so that this prize may be offered."

Soon all the classes at Robertsville began to work hard. Each class wanted to earn a prize.

When the carnival was held, Robertsville made a good profit. Students in homerooms that won prizes were happy, and those in homerooms that almost won were unhappy.

One member of a losing eighth-grade homeroom stopped Mr. Cotter in the hallway. He said, "Mr. Cotter, your contest was unfair. My homeroom worked hard. We earned a lot of money because we wanted to win a prize. We should get free movie tickets, even though we did not win."

Mr. Cotter was surprised. He replied, "Before the contest began, I announced the rules. The homeroom that won won according to the rules. When people compete for prizes, one group must win. Another group must lose. The contest was a fair one. I am sorry you lost. But you must learn to be a good loser if you are going to get along in our society."

Discussion Starters

COMPREHENSION

1. Why do teachers at Robertsville need money?

2. How does the principal decide to raise money?

3. Why does the principal announce a contest?

4. One student told the principal the contest was unfair. Why does the student believe the contest is unfair?

5. The principal said the contest was fair. Why does he believe the contest is fair?

RELATIONAL

6. When different persons or groups try to attain a goal and only one person or group can win, competition exists if everyone obeys the rules. Study this definition carefully. Did students at Robertsville compete with one another? Be prepared to defend your answer.

7. In this story, students compete for prizes. What other good things do students compete for in school?

8. Students frequently compete for good grades. What are some of the rules they must obey if they are to win?

VALUE/FEELING

9. Robertsville holds a carnival to raise money to start a new school program. Suppose you wanted to argue that this was a poor way to get money for a school. What might you say?

10. Is it good to raise money for school purposes by holding carnivals?

11. Students at Robertsville worked to earn prizes, not to start a new school program. Is there anything wrong with this?

The Cost of a Ten-Speed

Social Situation

Doug and Steve live next door to each other. They are good friends.

Doug and Steve attend the same school. Each morning they ride to school together on their bikes. Each Saturday, they ride their bikes to the mall.

This morning, Doug came for Steve early. He shouted, "Come on Steve. There's a yard sale just two blocks away. They're supposed to be selling a ten-speed bike. The ad said the bike is in excellent shape."

When Doug and Steve arrived at the yard sale, the bike was still there—and it was in excellent shape.

"It looks as though it has never been ridden," Steve told Doug.

Doug agreed. "I want to buy it if I can. I hope I've got enough money."

Steve asked the owner, "How much is the bike?"

"As much as I can sell it for," the owner laughed.

"I've only got forty-five dollars," Doug said. "I'll give you forty-five dollars for the bike."

The owner thought about the offer. "That's not bad. I might take forty-five dollars. Let me think about it for a bit."

Steve jumped in. "Give me a chance, will you?" He added, "I've got fifty dollars. Will you take fifty dollars for the bike?"

"You bet!" the owner replied. "Show me the money and you've got yourself a fine bike."

Steve bought the bike. He rode it all over his neighborhood showing it to the boys and girls with whom he and Doug play.

As for Doug, he spent most of the day in his house. Just before he went in, he had a few words for his friend, Steve.

"I'm going to look for a new buddy. You're a fine friend. You took that bike away from me. I hope it breaks down before you can even get it home. And don't you think I'm going to forget this. I'm going to remember what you did. I hope the bike was worth it."

DEALING WITH DILEMMAS

Discussion Starters

COMPREHENSION

1. Owning a good bike is important to both Doug and Steve. How do you know that this is true?

2. How much does the owner want for the new bike?

3. How much does Doug offer for the bike?

4. Steve offers more for the bike. How much more does he offer?

5. What does Steve do with the new bike?

6. What does Doug say to get even with Steve?

RELATIONAL

7. When an owner offers to sell something that more than one person wants, she hopes the persons who want what she has to sell will compete with one another. To what extent does this happen in the story?

8. When two or more persons compete for the same thing, they are supposed to obey certain rules. If any person who is competing breaks the rules, then conflict is likely. Does Steve break any rules that lead to conflict with Doug?

VALUE/FEELING

9. Should Steve have offered more for the bike than Doug could offer?

10. Steve bought the bike. How is this likely to hurt Steve and Doug one week later?

11. The owner wanted to sell his bike for the highest price. Was his behavior wrong?

Soccer Trouble

LOTS FOR SALE
555-3846

KEEP OUT
PRIVATE
PROPERTY

CONCEPTUAL FOCUS: POWER

Social Situation

Monica, Jennifer, Gabby, and Bridget all live on the same street. They are all in the sixth grade and want to be soccer players. When they get to high school, they all want to be on the varsity soccer team.

Last Christmas, each of the girls received a soccer ball. Since then, the girls have played soccer almost every day. They have used a vacant field at the end of the street.

The vacant field is a perfect place for the girls to play soccer. They can practice throw-ins and kicking. They can divide themselves into two teams and play a game. There are no windows to break, no flowers to trample, and no lawns to ruin. And smaller kids are not around to bother them either. They love to play in the vacant lot.

Things were great until last month. The girls went to the field as usual. When they got there, they found that the whole field had been mowed. There were big signs all over the place. The signs said: "Posted, No Trespassing," "Keep Out: Private Property," and "Lots for Sale: 555–3846."

Monica said, "Oh, no. Now we can't play in the field. We won't be able to play soccer any more."

Jennifer said, "Yes, we will. We'll play in Gabby's yard. She has the biggest yard of all of us."

Gabby said, "We can't do that. My father says we ruin the lawn. My mother says we ruin her flower beds."

Bridget said, "You're making a big deal out of this. They don't mean us. They mean hunters and those boys who are always riding their motorcycles across the field."

Gabby was suddenly happy. "That's right, Bridget. Good thinking. Let's stop talking and play a game."

The girls began to play. About thirty minutes later, Monica looked up and spotted a police car.

Monica turned to Gabby and said, "We're in trouble now."

Gabby's answer was, "Let's get out of here."

The girls ran home. They never went to the field to play again.

The lady who owned the field had exercised her right, or power, to have the field mowed. She had used her power to put up signs telling other people to stay out of the field. She had used her power to call the police. She could do this because she is a citizen and can demand police protection. As a property owner, she has controlled the behavior of Monica, Jennifer, Gabby, and Bridget.

Discussion Starters

COMPREHENSION

1. What is the favorite game of the girls in this story?

2. Why is the vacant lot at the end of their street a perfect place to play?

3. The vacant lot was not the only place the girls could have played. What other possible locations could they have used?

RELATIONAL

4. People sometimes do things to control the way we behave. When they do these things, we say that they are using power. Given this definition of power, how does the woman who owns the field try to control the girls?

5. Jennifer wants to play soccer in Gabby's yard. How does she try to use power over Gabby?

6. In this story, how does Gabby's father use power? Gabby's mother?

7. If a person can do bad things to you, they may control your behavior. This is true even if the person does nothing to hurt you. Given this definition of power, how does the police officer use power to control the four girls?

VALUE/FEELING

8. When the girls saw the signs in the field, what should they have done?

9. Suppose you were one of the four girls. If you were, what would you have done when you saw the signs?

10. Suppose you were one of the four girls. Assume the other girls got away but you did not. If this happened, what would you say to the police officer?

11. Assume the lady who owned the field saw you playing soccer and called the police. Did she do the right thing?

Surprise, Surprise!

Social Situation

Ms. Strachel teaches fifth grade. For the last three days, teaching has not been fun. Before school began on Friday, Ms. Strachel decided to review the week. She hoped she would be able to figure out what was wrong with her class. A summary of her review follows:

Monday—Things went well. Students worked without serious disruptions. Carl, a really nice boy, brought a new game to school—"Abr, Abr, Abr." None of the other children had seen the game before. They became quite excited. The only bad mom-ent was when the game had to be put away. For a moment, Carl was quite angry. All in all, it was a good day. For Monday, it was a very good day.

Tuesday—Things started fine. However, Wendy put a thumbtack on my chair during third period. I punished her by not allowing her to play Abr, Abr, Abr. During the afternoon, someone placed a rotting onion in my center desk drawer. I saw Larry wandering around my desk earlier and thought about not letting him play Abr, Abr, Abr. I didn't do this. Larry is too nice a boy to accuse just because he was near my desk. Tuesday was a bad day. I have never been happier to hear the dismissal bell for the day.

Wednesday—Things started bad and got no better. At the beginning, students refused to settle down and go to work. No matter what I tried, I could not get them to attend to what they were supposed to do. Before the day was over, I found nasty comments about me written on the blackboard and on the bulletin board. I suspected Michael and Joan, but this made no sense to me. Michael and Joan are pleasant students. I have always thought they liked me as a teacher.

Thursday—Carl was late. However, he was very polite as he handed me his tardy note. This made me feel good. I needed a boost. I thought, "Maybe things will go better today." But this was not to be. Again students did not work well. In addition, I had to break up a fight between Carl and Joan. It seems that Michael and Joan took Carl's new game home with them last night. The corner of the box in which the game is kept was torn. Carl accused Michael and Joan. But Michael and Joan said that Larry had done it the night before. After the fight, students were more restless than they had been before.

Ms. Strachel reviewed her notes. Suddenly, and to her surprise, she began to understand what had been happening in her fifth-grade class. Carl was controlling access to a new game that the other

DEALING WITH DILEMMAS

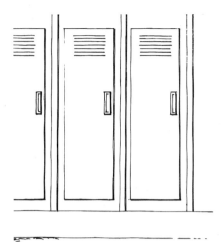

children wanted to play.

She thought, "He probably asked Wendy to put a thumbtack on my chair. He encouraged Larry to put an onion in my desk. He offered to let Michael and Joan take the game home for a night if they put remarks on the blackboard and bulletin board. It was Carl who disrupted the class for almost a whole week."

Ms. Strachel has been hurt by the power of one of her students. This student, Carl, has the power to make teaching almost impossible for Ms. Strachel.

"Who would have thought it?" Ms. Strachel smiled as she began to consider how she would handle the situation, now that she understood what had been happening.

Discussion Starters

COMPREHENSION

1. Who brings a new game to school?

2. When does Carl decide to hurt Ms. Strachel?

3. How does Carl hurt Ms. Strachel?

4. On one day, enough information becomes available for Ms. Strachel to know that Carl is the cause of her problems. Which day is this?

5. How many students does Carl get to help him?

6. How many students does Carl hurt?

RELATIONAL

7. Carl can influence students like Larry, Michael, and Joan to behave in ways they do not wish to behave. This means he has power over them. What information in the story supports this?

8. Ms. Strachel will need to use power to influence Carl to behave as a student should behave. What can a teacher do in order to have power over the behavior of students?

VALUE/FEELING

9. How does Carl hurt his classmates in this story?

10. What should Ms. Strachel do about Wendy, Larry, Michael, and Joan?

11. What should Ms. Strachel do about Carl's behavior?

Working for a Wagon

Social Situation

Rose and Emily wanted a wagon that they could use around their neighborhood. They rode their bikes down to the mall. The cheapest wagon that they could find cost $51.95. It was bright red and shiny white. It had a built-in tape deck and places to store their stuff. It was just what they wanted.

Rose and Emily rode home. Each went to her house and counted her money. Emily had $12.55. Rose had $11.79. When they put their money together, they didn't have enough to buy the wagon.

Rose decided to see how much they still needed. She worked two problems:

$ 12.55	Emily's money
$ 11.79	My money
$ 24.34	We have this much money
$ 51.95	What the wagon costs
$ 24.34	How much we have
$ 27.61	Money needed to buy the wagon

Emily said, "Let's see if we can borrow the money we need from our parents. They have enough money to give us what we need."

Rose replied, "My parents told me they won't lend any money to us for things we want to buy."

Emily said, "Let's see if we can arrange to do some jobs around the neighborhood. Maybe we can earn enough money to buy the wagon."

Rose said, "That's a great idea. Let's talk to some of the neighbors."

They went first to talk to Mrs. Pardo. Mrs. Pardo wanted to have her front yard raked. She promised to pay the girls $4.00 to rake her front yard.

Mr. Smith wanted his lawn mowed. He offer-ed to pay the girls $6.50 if they did a good job.

Mr. Washington offered to pay the girls $5.00 if they would clean his swimming pool.

Mrs. Camp wanted to have her car washed. She said she could only pay $3.00.

Rose's mother said, "I would like to have the outside of the windows washed. I can pay you and Emily $5.00."

Emily's mother also wanted to help the girls. She said, "The carport and utility room are a mess. If you clean them, I will pay you $5.00."

Emily and Rose made a list of all these jobs. They wanted to see if they would have enough money to buy the new wagon. Their list looked liked this:

$ 4.00	Mrs. Pardo yard raked
$ 6.50	Mr. Smith lawn mowed
$ 5.00	Mr. Washington swimming pool cleaned
$ 3.00	Mrs. Camp car washed
$ 5.00	Rose's Mom windows
$ 5.00	Emily's Mom carport
$ 28.50	TOTAL

Rose said, "We'll have enough money, and we'll have almost a dollar left."

The girls worked hard for the next week. They raked Mrs. Pardo's yard, mowed Mr. Smith's lawn, cleaned Mr. Washington's pool, and washed Mrs. Camp's car.

By Saturday morning, two jobs were left to be done. The windows must be washed for Rose's mother, and the carport must be cleaned for Emily's mother. Rose and Emily were up bright and early. First, they did the windows. After lunch, they went to work on Emily's carport. By four o'clock, they were finished.

Emily's mother said, "You girls have worked hard. I'll take you to get your new wagon."

When they reached the mall, Rose and Emily were very excited. They rushed into the store. They quickly spotted the wagon they wanted.

Emily's mother said, "Just a minute. Look at the price."

Rose looked at the sign. It was new. It read: "Deluxe Wagon: Only $59.95!!"

Emily said, "This can't be right. It's the same wagon that we saw Saturday. It's supposed to be $51.95."

Rose said, "That's right!"

Emily's mother said, "Let's ask the manager."

When they found the store manager he said, "I'm sorry. Last week the wagon cost $51.95. This week it costs $59.95. Our prices just keep going up."

Emily said, "That's a dirty trick."

Rose said, "That is not fair."

Both girls were disappointed. They had counted up all their money. They had started with $24.34. They had earned $28.50. They did not have enough to pay the new price.

$ 24.34	Money to start with
$ 28.50	Money earned
$ 52.84	All our money

Both Emily and Rose were unhappy. They had earned money to buy a wagon. While they were earning the money, the wagon became more costly. Both girls felt like crying.

Discussion Starters

COMPREHENSION

1. What did Rose and Emily want to buy?

2. How much money did the wagon cost?

3. How did the girls use their knowledge of mathematics?

4. How many tasks did Emily and Rose do to save up for the wagon?

5. In terms of being hurt, how much did wanting the wagon cost Rose and Emily?

RELATIONAL

6. Each time Rose and Emily finished a job, they were more able to buy the wagon. Their ability to buy was more like what they wanted it to be. This means that they were less and less deprived of what they wanted. What does being less deprived mean?

7. Rose and Emily went into the store believing they would leave with the new wagon. Because the wagon now cost more, they could not afford to buy it. Why did they want to cry this time, but not the first time?

VALUE/FEELING

8. Suppose Emily's mother wants to help the two girls feel better. If she wants to help them, what should she do?

9. Suppose the store manager wants to help the two girls feel better. What should he do?

10. Suppose you were Rose or Emily. What would you do?

$udden Wealth

Social Situation

Ogma is a very small country located on the planet Oktu. Ogma has always been a poor country. It has always had very few good schools. There have not been enough hospitals to care for the ill.

For a long time, the people of Ogma have wanted to build enough good schools so that all children may be educated. Ogmans have also wanted to build more hospitals to care for the sick. Until last year, this seemed impossible.

Last year, a corporation found a major oil field under Lake Ogma. The money from the oil reserves will increase the money available to those who govern Ogma.

Ogmans spoke confidently about using the money from the oil to build more schools and hospitals—the two goals they had wished but had not expected to achieve.

Ogmans were disappointed last week, though, when the Governor of Ogma spoke.

"My friends, I am aware that you expect my government to use money derived from the sale of our oil to build new schools and hospitals.

"I am sincerely sorry to disappoint you. Nevertheless, I must be honest with you. Our population is growing rapidly. This rapid population growth means that we will have to be more selective than we were in choosing who gets to go to school. This means that fewer of our ill will be able to secure hospital treatment."

Ogmans were very disappointed. Some groups talked about starting a revolution. In fact, the Ogmans felt that they had been deprived and cheated. The Ogmans were suffering from a condition of relative deprivation.

In this case, the expectations of the Ogmans—to have more schools and hospitals—increased. The capability for securing more schools and hospitals decreased because of rapid population growth. Whenever the expectations of a person or group increase and the abilities of a person or group to attain these expectations decline, a condition of relative deprivation occurs.

Discussion Starters

COMPREHENSION

1. Where does this story take place?

2. What are some of the things that Ogmans want?

3. What makes Ogmans believe they can have more good things than they used to have?

4. Ogmans are told that they cannot have the good things they expect to have. Why?

RELATIONAL

5. If expectations grow faster than a group's ability to have the good things members of the groups expect, persons are likely to feel deprived. Is this statement true for this story?

6. If a group expects more than it can have, the group is likely to feel deprived. Describe at least one situation in which you have been deprived.

VALUE/FEELING

7. Should the Ogmans start a revolution?

8. The governor said, "I must be honest with you." Assume the governor wishes to remain in power. If this is true, did the governor do the right thing?

9. Pretend you are the ruler of the Ogmans. If you were, how would you try to help them feel better?

10. The governor says that population growth is costing Ogmans a chance for good schools and good health care. Should those who rule or govern force citizens to control population? Defend your response.

From the Teacher's Perspective

To use a standard format of structured dilemma, (1) assign the dilemma and remind students of the topic, concept, or idea that is currently being studied; (2) inform students that the stimulus situation is relevant to the current focus of study; and (3) indicate that once students have had an opportunity to study the social situation, they will be expected to respond, personally and publicly, to directions and questions.

Next, allow students a period of time in which to study the resource. This should be a quiet time in which no talking or excess movement occurs. You must be especially alert, for it is the teacher who is most likely to disrupt student attention by talking, moving about, or engaging in some other distracting activity. The importance of this period of quiet study will be emphasized for each of the five formats of structured dilemma presented.

When students have studied the resource, distribute the discussion starters and ask students to write answers to the questions and directions. Do not distribute discussion starters before students study the social situation, to keep them from looking for answers to the discussion starters. When students are writing their initial reactions to discussion starters, it is important that they work alone.

Once students have written responses to the discussion starters, use these questions and directions to ascertain that students have (1) comprehended the social situation; (2) framed relationships between the social situation and the current focus of study; and (3) reacted personally in terms of their values and feelings toward the social situation. You do not have to use all the questions in the discussion starters, and you should use questions that you have developed. Each classroom is different, so it is unlikely that you will use the questions found in the discussion starters in the same order as they are written. The questions are intended to be a guide. Your role at this stage is to provide for comprehension, analysis, and personalization, doing whatever is necessary to secure these instructional ends.

As students respond, employ two skills consistently: wait-time and probing. These will facilitate, clarify, and complete student responses. Without them, students may not be able to respond to questions completely.

Finally, summarize what you believe students have learned and introduce the next learning activity.

Each of the five phases of usage are important. The initial assignment tends to focus student attention and establish a learning set. The study time creates optimum conditions for students to acquire and begin to process information. Asking students to write answers enhances the likelihood that they will participate in the discussion that follows. The discussion of individual student responses enables students to contrast how they have reasoned with how other students have reasoned and provides both the teacher and other students with the chance to challenge students to think in new ways. The teacher summary at the end helps students to isolate those aspects of the learning activity that are worthy of being remembered and/or used.

On Your Own

Most standard instructional resources may be converted into structured dilemmas. To accomplish this, take the following steps:

1. Define the focus of study within which you intend to use the structured dilemma.

2. Select a reading, visual, or audio resource that is relevant to the current focus of study. Alternatively, you may choose to paraphrase such a resource or write your own social situation.

3. Write four, five, or six questions that students may use in order to test their understanding of the social situation. (Conventions for doing this were presented at the beginning of this chapter, in the section entitled "Description.")

4. Write two, three, or four relational questions that will help students seek out relationships between the social situation and their current focus of study. (See "Descriptions.")

5. Write two to five value/feeling questions that will require students to express personal preferences and feelings about the social situation. (See "Descriptions.")

2

THE FORCED-CHOICE FORMAT OF STRUCTURED DILEMMA

Functions

When an individual or group needs to make a decision between two courses of action, one good and one bad, it is seldom difficult to do so. Many important decisions, however, do not offer easy choices. Individuals and members of groups frequently choose the greater good at the expense of sacrificing other good things, or they must opt for the lesser evil to avoid actions that are even worse. The forced-choice format of structured dilemma provides situations in which students, as individuals and as members of a group—seek the greater good or the lesser evil.

Description

The forced-choice format of structured dilemma contains four components: a social context, a list of options, an individual decision sheet, and a group decision sheet.

The social situation confronts students with a situation within which an individual or a group must make a decision from a limited number of options; hence the name "forced-choice." The social situation establishes the constraints within which a decision is to be made. It is also desirable to provide sufficient information for students to assume the roles of persons who are presented in the social situation, i.e., to engage in role-playing.

The second component is a short list of options, usually three to five in number. These are the only policies that students are to consider in making an appropriate decision for the social situation. These options are homogeneous: all of the options are either positive or negative. This, in effect, structures a situation in which students must choose the greater good at the price of sacrificing other good options; or students must choose the lesser evil in order to avoid other and worse options. This situation does not allow students the convenient out—selecting something that is either totally good or totally bad. Students are forced to sometimes select a seemingly undesirable option.

The third component is an individual decision sheet. This is to be completed by students working independently before the group discussion of the relative merits of the options. This decision sheet elicits two forms of student behavior. First, each student selects the option he or she believes is best for the situation given. Second, each student explains why he or she believes that the option selected is best. Once this decision sheet has been completed, individual student's reactions become an integral component of the decision-making exercise.

The fourth component is a group decision sheet. Groups of four or five students work together in order to complete this decision sheet. The group decision sheet is intended to cue three forms of student behavior. Students share their individual reactions with one another and reexamine the social situation at the focus of the activity. They use communication and persuasion skills to seek consensus on one decision and one rationale that they, as a group, are willing to share with other members of the class.

Classroom Examples

Six examples of the forced-choice format of structured dilemma are provided here. Study at least four of these examples in order to develop the understanding necessary to use the decision sheets written in this format or to write your own decision sheets.

A VISITOR IN LIMESTONE

CONCEPTUAL FOCUS: CONFLICT

Social Situation

Mayor Carson has been mayor of Limestone for more than fifteen years. Limestone is a beautiful little town. It is located in a high valley in the mountains of the Northwest. It is surrounded on all sides by a beautiful forest. A sparkling clear river full of fish runs by the town.

Limestone has a small population. Each year, more people leave because there are few jobs. Besides, jobs in the cities pay more money. Limestone has many empty buildings. Some people say, "The town of Limestone is dying."

Mayor Carson hates to see her town become smaller and smaller. She knows that she needs to find some way to keep people from moving away.

Yesterday, Mayor Carson found one possible answer. A man who works for a company that makes clothes came to see Mayor Carson. The visitor said, "My company wants to build a factory in Limestone. Our factory will make shirts and socks. We will hire local people to work in this factory."

There is one big problem. While making the socks and shirts, the new factory will produce wastewater. The factory will take in water from the river to use during manufacturing. After its use, the water will be treated to remove the pollutants that the federal government requires to be removed. However, the water is very warm and full of things the river never contained before. In other areas, this type of waste water has made rivers turn murky and has killed many fish.

Mayor Carson is undecided. She wants the factory because the people of Limestone need jobs. She wants to protect the river because it is one of the things that makes Limestone a fine place to live. Mayor Carson wants both of these things. Her two wishes are in conflict.

THE FORCED-CHOICE FORMAT OF STRUCTURED DILEMMA

Options

Mayor Carson does not like to feel worried. She knows that she needs to make a decision. Finally, she makes a list of the four things that she might do in this situation:

1. I can say that we do not want the factory, but then the people of my town will have to leave to find jobs.

2. I can say that we are pleased to have the factory, but then the river may be ruined.

3. I can call a town meeting and let the people of Limestone make the decision, but this may cause hard feelings between neighbors.

4. I can encourage the factory to locate down stream from Limestone, but is this fair to the towns that are downstream from Limestone?

INDIVIDUAL DECISION SHEET

Use this decision sheet to record what you would do if you were Mayor Carson. Complete this decision sheet by yourself. Do not discuss it with anyone until you have completed it.

Select the best thing that Mayor Carson can do in this situation. Indicate your choice by using a check mark (✔).

_____Tell the visitor that you do not want the factory.

_____Tell the visitor that you want the factory.

_____Call a town meeting, and let the people decide.

_____Ask the visitor to locate the factory downstream from the town.

I believe my answer is best, because

_____

_____

_____

_____

GROUP DECISION SHEET

Imagine that you and the other members of your group are the town council of Limestone. Mayor Carson has asked your group to decide what she should do about the factory. Try to agree on one answer without voting.

As a group, we believe the mayor should

_____Welcome the new factory.

_____Oppose the new factory.

_____Call a town meeting.

_____Try to locate the factory downstream.

We believe our recommendation is best, because

_____

_____

_____

Group members making this decision are

_____

_____

_____

Two Men of High Honor

MILLTOWN BAPTIST CHURCH

Social Situation

For the purpose of this exercise, you are to imagine that you are a Baptist minister. You have just become the new minister at the Milltown Baptist Church. Right away, you discover that some of the men are doing evil things. You want to stop these men.

Milltown is located near the Smokey Mountains. It serves the needs of farmers and mill workers.

Milltown is a very small town. There is a single gas station, where you can get gas or repairs for your car. There is a single pharmacy, where you can fill prescriptions or buy over-the-counter medications. There are two stores where you can buy clothing, food, and other items. These are called general stores.

Most of the people who live in Milltown are very poor. Most of them work in a mill where paper is made. They are not paid very well. They almost never get a raise. These workers cannot afford to go to the city to buy their clothes and food. The nearest mall is more than 150 miles away, over poor roads.

The farmers who live in the country around Milltown are also quite poor. Their farms are rocky and hilly, but they do sell one crop for money. This cash crop is tobacco.

Besides tobacco, the farmers grow much of their own food. Like the poor people who live in Milltown itself, the farmers cannot afford to go to the city to buy food and clothing.

Mr. Bray and Mr. Slicker own the two general stores where food and clothing are sold. Mr. Bray's store is at the north end of Milltown. It is called the Northside General Store.

Mr. Slicker's store is located at the south end of Milltown. It is called the Milltown General Store.

Mr. Bray and Mr. Slicker are important people in Milltown. Mr. Bray is the mayor of the town. Mr. Slicker is a member of the school board. Each man wants to be a good citizen.

Mr. Bray and Mr. Slicker go to the same church, the one in which you preach. They are both leaders in the church. Both teach Sunday school classes. Both are deacons. Each man wants to be a good Christian. Mr. Bray and Mr. Slicker are both members of the Milltown Leadership Club. The Leadership Club is the most important group in Milltown. Those who own businesses in Milltown are members. The school principal and the school superintendent are members. Mr. Bray and Mr. Slicker are proud to be members of the Milltown Leadership Club.

Mr. Bray and Mr. Slicker make good money in their stores. Most of the men and women who work in the paper mill buy their food and clothes from Mr. Bray and Mr. Slicker.

Years ago, Mr. Bray and Mr. Slicker agreed that they would always do certain things. Among these were the following:

1. We will never have special prices on household goods. Sugar, coffee, salt, bread, flour, shortening, and spices will cost the same every day.
2. We will never have weekend special prices for hamburger meat, steaks,

hams, turkeys, or chickens. All meat will be the same price every day.

3. We will never put work shoes, work clothes, coats, or other clothing on sale. All our customers will always pay the full price for such goods.

4. We will never give rebates or double coupons to customers who shop with us. We could pass part of this cost on to our customers. However, since we would have to pay part of the cost, this would cut down on the profits we want to make.

5. Each time we cash a weekly payroll check or a social security check we will charge one dollar. However, neither of us will charge our friends or members of the Leadership Club for this service. Only workers and farmers will be charged.

These rules mean that the mill workers and the poor farmers must pay more for their food, clothing, and supplies. The rules mean that Mr. Bray and Mr. Slicker will make more money. The rules also mean that some children may go hungry and cold.

Mr. Bray and Mr. Slicker have never signed an agreement. They trust one another and have cooperated with one another for a long time. They have made good money.

One day when Mr. Bray was talking to Mr. Slicker, Mr. Bray said, "Shucks, Mr. Slicker, we don't need to sign anything. We're both honorable men and civic leaders."

Mr. Slicker responded, "I agree. Good men like us will always keep our word."

When you, as the new Baptist minister, become aware of how Mr. Bray and Mr. Slicker do business, you are shocked. You believe that each person should treat all others as he or she would wish to be treated. You feel that you must do something to keep Mr. Bray and Mr. Slicker from mistreating the poor workers and farmers.

At the same time, you know that Mr. Bray and Mr. Slicker are important members of your church. Were they to leave your church, you would lose their weekly offering. The loss of this money would hurt the church. You make a list of four things that you might do. From this list of four possibilities, you intend to chose one.

Options

1. Preach a sermon on the evil of greed and the virtue of charity.

2. Condemn Mr. Bray and Mr. Slicker in a sermon next Sunday, and ask them to change their rules.

3. Talk to Mr. Bray and Mr. Slicker privately, but do nothing to embarrass them publicly.

4. Organize the millworkers, and help them start their own general store.

DEALING WITH DILEMMAS

INDIVIDUAL DECISION SHEET

Use this decision sheet to record what you would do if you were the new Baptist minister. Complete this decision sheet by yourself. Do not discuss it with anyone until you have completed it.

Select the best thing that you, as the Baptist minister, can do in this situation. Indicate your choice by using a check mark (✔).

_____Preach a sermon. Stress the need to be good citizens.

_____Preach a sermon. Condemn Mr. Bray's and Mr. Slicker's actions.

_____Talk privately to Mr. Bray and Mr. Slicker. Don't say anything publicly.

_____Help the mill workers start their own general store.

Suppose you were asked by another minister to defend you choice. How would you convince the minister that your choice is best?

_____

_____

_____

_____

_____

_____

GROUP DECISION SHEET DIRECTIONS

To fill out this decision sheet, all members of your group must pretend that a number of things are true.

1. All members of your group attend the new minister's church. He has asked you to help him decide what to do.

2. All members of your group like the new minister. You want him to do well in your town.

3. All members of your group believe in the golden rule, "Do unto others as you would have them do unto you."

4. All members of your group believe that the church needs the money that Mr. Bray and Mr. Slicker give each Sunday.

5. All members of your group believe that Mr. Bray and Mr. Slicker are cooperating to do a bad thing.

6. All members of your group want your church to be a good church. You want the church to help all the people who live and shop in Milltown.

Keep these things in mind as you complete this decision sheet. Also, keep in mind that you are to agree to the one best thing that the minister can do. Try to agree without voting.

GROUP DECISION SHEET

We believe the best thing our minister can do is to

Preach a sermon telling people it is wrong to be greedy. Tell people it is good to be kind and help the poor.

Preach a sermon telling people the kinds of rules that Mr. Bray and Mr. Slicker use to make a good profit. Tell people that Mr. Bray and Mr. Slicker should stop doing these bad things.

Talk to Mr. Bray and Mr. Slicker, but do not make them angry. The church needs the money.

Start a new store and tell people that Milltown needs a store that is run by people who want to help the poor.

We believe our choice is best, because

_____

_____

_____

Group members making this decision are

_____

_____

_____

Welcome Home, Mr. Willy

Social Situation

Mascot has always been a small town. The people who live in the country around Mascot are truck farmers. They raise vegetables and take them to the city about sixty miles away. They sell most of their vegetables to grocery stores located in the city.

Mascot has a large hardware store. The hardware store sells tools, fertilizer, and home repair items. It also sells electric stoves, refrigerators, and television sets.

Mascot has one service station. The owner of the service station is also a mechanic. He fixes cars, tractors, and trucks.

Mascot also has one grocery store. In addition to food, the store also sells work clothes and shoes.

Unless the people of Mascot can find what they want in these stores, they must go to the city to shop.

Recently, a man who grew up in Mascot returned home. His name is Mr. Willy.

Mr. Willy moved to the city when he was twenty-five years old. For the last twenty years, he has worked for a television store in the city as a repairman.

Soon after returning to Mascot, Mr. Willy told his friends he was going to start a new store. "I will sell refrigerators, freezers, stoves, air conditioners, stereos, VCRs, and television sets. With my training, I will be able to service what I sell. I believe the town of Mascot needs a store whose only business is appliances."

When Mr. Schmidt, who owns the hardware store, was told, he was surprised. "Imagine that," he said.

"What will you do, Mr. Schmidt?" he was asked.

"We'll see," Mr. Schmidt answered.

Mr. Schmidt thought of several things he might do when Mr. Willy opened his new store. The things Mr. Schmidt began to think about are the options that follow.

Options

1. "I might sell appliances for what they cost me. Then Mr. Willy could make no profit. Soon he would have to close his store. Then, I could raise the cost of my appliances and make a good profit."

2. "I might ask Mr. Willy to buy my stock of appliances. Who knows? What I sell may be more trouble than it is worth. If I sell my stock to Mr. Willy, I can put my effort into selling hardware goods and services."

3. "I might hire a serviceman to work in my hardware store. This will enable me to offer the same services Mr. Willy will offer. Since my business is established, Mr. Willy will probably make too little money to stay in business."

4. "My customers depend on me for tools, seed, and fertilizer. Many of them buy these things on credit and then pay me when they sell their crops. They even borrow money from me in emergencies. I'll let these people know that I expect them to be loyal customers. If I catch them buying from Mr. Willy, I'll make it tough for them."

INDIVIDUAL DECISION SHEET

• •

Complete this decision sheet before you discuss it with other members of your class. Select the one thing you would do if you were Mr. Schmidt. Mark your choice with a check mark (✔).

_____Sell my goods at cost, and drive Mr. Willy out of business.

_____Try to sell my appliances to Mr. Willy.

_____Hire a serviceman to work in the hardware store.

_____Force my customers to be loyal to me.

As Mr. Schmidt, I believe my choice is best because

_____

_____

_____

_____

_____

GROUP DECISION SHEET

Work with members of your group to complete this exercise. As a group, select the one best policy that Mr. Schmidt should use. Try to reach an agreement without voting. When you have finished, you will be allowed to share the decision your group makes with other members of the class.

We believe Mr. Schmidt should

_____ Sell his goods at cost and drive Mr. Willy out of business.

_____ Sell his appliances to Mr. Willy.

_____ Hire his own serviceman.

_____ Force customers who owe him favors to do business at his hardware store.

If asked to defend our choice, we would say

_____

_____

_____

Group members making this decision are

_____

_____

_____

On Cheating and Being Fair

Social Situation

Last Friday, Ms. Douglas was unable to teach her eighth-grade American history class. The principal called a substitute teacher who took Ms. Douglas's place.

Ms. Douglas told the substitute teacher, "You should have an easy day. Almost every Friday, I ask the students to take a weekly quiz. This helps my students to see how well they are learning American history. This also helps me plan what I will do the following week."

The substitute teacher did as Ms. Douglas had asked her to do. She had students take a weekly quiz.

Today, Ms. Douglas graded all the papers from her fifth-period American history class. After grading the papers, Ms. Douglas notices that four students had answers that were identical. Ms. Douglas is certain that these four students had cheated on the quiz.

Ms. Douglas does not know what to do in this situation. She has thought of a number of things she might do, and these are listed at the right as options.

Options

1. Ms. Douglas might offer to reward anyone who tells her how the four students cheated.

2. Ms. Douglas might throw all the papers away. She could tell her class the papers are lost and give them another test.

3. Ms. Douglas might tell her class she believes a number of students cheated. She could then refuse to record any of the grades in her record book.

4. Ms. Douglas might keep all members of her class after school. She could give them a grade of zero. This would set an example for all her students.

5. Ms. Douglas might say nothing and record the grades. Then in the future, she can avoid asking a substitute to give tests in her classes.

INDIVIDUAL
DECISION
SHEET

Suppose you really like and respect Ms. Douglas. Suppose that she asks you to advise her. Given these two conditions, complete this decision sheet. Do this by yourself.

Mark your choice with a check mark (✔). Ms. Douglas should

_____Pretend that all the papers have been lost.

_____Refuse to record any of the grades.

_____Keep the entire class after school.

_____Record all grades and say nothing else.

_____Offer to reward an informer.

If asked to justify my advice, I would say

_____

_____

_____

_____

_____

GROUP DECISION SHEET

Work with members of your group to complete this decision sheet. Try to reach an agreement about what Ms. Douglas should do. Do not vote.

We believe Ms. Douglas should

_____Pretend that all the papers have been lost.

_____Refuse to record any of the grades.

_____Keep the entire class after school.

_____Record all grades and say nothing.

_____Offer to reward an informer.

We believe this choice is best because

_____

_____

_____

_____

Persons responsible for making this decision are

_____

_____

_____

The End of the Bench

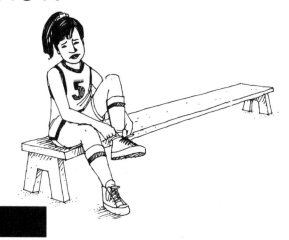

Social Situation

Kelly loved sports. She especially loved to play basketball.

Kelly was not a good athlete. She was not fast; she did not shoot the basketball very well; and she did not have great coordination. However, she was a very hard worker.

In the sixth grade, Kelly went out for the basketball team. She barely made the team. Most of the time she sat on the end of the bench and watched the other girls play.

Kelly decided she would work very hard to get ready for next season. All summer long she practiced. She practiced chest passes, bounce passes, jump shots, and free throws. She even practiced defensive moves. She wanted to be able to play defense as well as she could. Kelly thought the coach would let her play more if she saw how good a defender she had become. Kelly even played pick-up basketball games at the playground to practice her new skills.

When the next season arrived, Kelly tried out for the seventh-grade basketball team. She was certain that she would be a starter.

However, over the summer, the other girls had also improved. They ran faster, shot better, and passed the ball and played defense with more skill. Although Kelly was improved, the other girls had improved even more rapidly than she.

The coach said to Kelly , "I know how hard you have worked and how much you have improved. I want to keep you on the team but you'll probably end up back down at the end of the bench."

Kelly barely held back her tears.

The coach continued, "I know you must be very disappointed. I will understand if you want to call it quits."

Options

Kelly could think of only three things that she might do. These were

1. To quit the team and do something else.

2. To stay on the team and accept that she will be on the end of the bench and seldom play.

3. To stay on the team, work harder, and hope the coach changes her mind.

THE FORCED-CHOICE FORMAT OF STRUCTURED DILEMMA

INDIVIDUAL DECISION SHEET

Work by yourself to complete this decision sheet. Later, you will have an opportunity to share your answers with the other members of a small group. As you answer, pretend you are Kelly and want to play basketball very much.

Of the three options that follow, select the one thing you would do if you were Kelly. Mark your choice with a check mark (✔). Kelly should

_____Quit the team and do something else.

_____Stay on the team and accept that she will be on the end of the bench and seldom play.

_____Stay on the team, work harder, and hope the coach changes her mind.

I believe this is my best choice because

_____

_____

_____

_____

_____

GROUP DECISION SHEET

Work together on this assignment. First, find out how each member of your group responded to the individual decision sheet. Then try to agree as a group on the best choice that Kelly might make. Afterward, you will be expected to share your decision with other members of the class.

We believe Kelly should

_____Quit the team and do something else.

_____Stay on the team and accept that she will be on the end of the bench and seldom play.

_____Stay on the team, work harder, and hope the coach changes her mind.

We believe this choice is best because

_____

_____

_____

_____

_____

Group members making this decision are

_____

_____

_____

And the Winner Is...

Social Situation

This is the last night of the local science fair. Tomorrow the judges will make one last check before deciding on the winners. There will be only one winner in each category, and the winner will go to the regional contest.

Last year, Keri won the contest in her category. This year, she expected the same easy victory. However, the other displays are as good as hers. She even overheard one of the judges talking about how hard it was to make a decision among all the fine projects.

After the closing of the displays, everyone was ordered to leave the hall. The night watchman was instructed not to touch any of the projects.

An hour after she arrived home, Keri couldn't remember whether she had turned off a button on her display. Her mother took her back to the hall. The watchman allowed her to enter the hall to check the display. The button had not been turned off.

After checking her display, Keri suddenly realized that she could easily win if small things should suddenly happen to the other displays. Keri changed the other displays.

The next day, Keri was announced as the winner of her category. However, as two of the young scientists began taking their projects down, they noticed that something was wrong.

"Someone messed with my project!" they both yelled out.

After an extensive investigation, Keri admitted altering the displays the previous evening. As a result, her prize was awarded to another contestant.

As the chief judge announced the name of the new winner, he addressed the audience:

"We are not upset with Keri as a person, but we are bothered by what she did. Her actions are what concern us now. The problem is how to prevent this from occurring again. A number of options are available to us. I want the audience to help me determine which of these options is the best possible one for us to take in the future."

• •

Options

1. Prevent Keri from ever entering another contest as a lesson to other students.

2. Award no prizes to anyone, but continue to have the science displays.

3. Continue to hold the contest, but have more prizes in each category.

4. Increase the punishment for those caught changing the displays of another person.

5. Hold no more contests or displays.

INDIVIDUAL DECISION SHEET

Assume you are a member of the audience that was asked to help the judge make a decision. Working alone, select the option you consider to be the best. In a few minutes, you will share your responses with the rest of a small group.

Of the three options that follow, select the one thing you would do. Mark your choice with a check mark (✔).

_____Prevent Keri from ever entering another contest as a lesson to other students.

_____Award no prizes to anyone, but continue to have the science displays.

_____Continue to hold the contest, but have more prizes in each category.

_____Increase the punishment for those caught changing the displays of another person.

_____Hold no more contests or displays.

I believe my answer is best, because

_____

_____

_____

_____

_____

GROUP DECISION SHEET

Work together on this assignment. First, find out how each member of your group responded to the individual decision sheet. Then try to agree as a group on the best choice that can be made. Afterward, you will be expected to share your decision with other members of the class.

We believe the best response would be to

_____Prevent Keri from ever entering another contest as a lesson to other students.

_____Award no prizes to anyone, but continue to have the science displays.

_____Continue to hold the contest, but have more prizes in each category.

_____Increase the punishment for those caught changing the displays of another person.

_____Hold no more contests or displays.

We believe this choice is best because

_____

_____

_____

_____

_____

Group members responsible for making this decision are

_____

_____

_____

_____

From the Teacher's Perspective

When using a forced-choice format of structured dilemma, initiate the activity by reviewing the current focus of study—the topic, theme, concept, or idea that is being studied. Then indicate that the dilemma is related to the current focus of study. Also indicate that individuals and groups must sometimes choose the greater good or the lesser evil. Behaviors such as these tend to establish a learning set according to which students perceive purpose in what they are asked to do.

With a learning set established, distribute the social situation and the limited list of options. Ask students to study the situation and the list of options carefully; also tell them that they will need to comprehend these two components because such understanding is critical to the completion of the activity.

Then give the students time to study the social situation and the list of options. During study time, you should maintain a learning environment in which there is no unnecessary movement or talk. Although this point was stressed in Chapter 1, it is important to note again that you must act as your own watchdog in order to avoid one of the prime sources of disruptive behavior, the teacher.

Once the students have studied the social situation, ascertain that they have comprehended it and can relate it to the current focus of study. In order to do this, use comprehension and relational directions and questions phrased according to the conventions presented in Chapter 1. At this point, discourage any effort that students make to express judgmental statements about the limited set of options.

Next, distribute the individual decision sheet. Tell students that they are to complete this decision sheet prior to discussing it with other students, and that once they have completed it, they will have a chance to share opinions with other members of a small group.

When students have completed the individual decision sheet, divide the class into small decision-making groups of three to five. It is important here to obtain a good mix of students that cuts across informal classroom groups and cliques. Randomly select a student and then give all students a number by counting off: "one," "two," "three," "four," "five." (Use as many numbers as there are members of each group.) Continue until each student has been assigned a number. All students assigned the same number become a group. There are other methods of accomplishing random selection. The one presented is meant to serve as an example, not as an indication of the only method.

Before students move into their groups to complete the decision sheet, explain the assignment. Stress that students are to begin by sharing individual reactions and then to seek consensus. This explanation helps curtail confusion and unnecessary noise.

Group work sometimes takes a significant period of time to get started. During the initial moments in a group, the group is assigning roles rather than working on the assigned task. (Often the students get frustrated, and the groups disintegrate into gossip sessions.) The teacher can assist the students by assigning the roles ahead of time. For example, one group member becomes the group "recorder," another member the "reader," and another the "reporter." In this manner the groups initial "negotiated" roles can be handled for them. This assignment of roles can also be accomplished assigning numbers within each group, so that all "ones" are readers, "twos" recorders, and "threes" reporters. Other methods of group and role assignment include the use of playing cards (the suit decides the group, the card value decides the role) and the use of poker chips (color determines group, symbol on the chip decides the role).

The students in each group begin by sharing their individual reactions to the social situation. With this accomplished, students seek consensus on the best option and a rationale for the selection. During this period of interaction, you should move about the room, quietly monitoring student performance. Monitor each group with at least four questions in mind:

1. Are all members of the group participating?
2. Do members of the group share personal reactions?
3. Do members of the group seek consensus on the best opinion?
4. Do members of the group seek consensus on the best criterion or explanation for the option they selected?

Intervene if necessary, but avoid becoming a party to group discussions whenever you judge them to be functioning successfully.

Close the activity by doing at least three things. First, ask one member of each group to share that group's work with other members of the class. (Was a reporter assigned?) Second, review some of the important ways in which the activity is relevant to the current focus of study in the class. Third, provide the students with an opportunity to practice metacognition. This can be accomplished by raising questions such as: What do you think about your decision-making process? Would you change anything about it? If so, what? This type of question will help students make explicit parts of decision making that are often left implicit.

Using group work in the classroom has been shown to be an effective learning tool. However, in many classrooms, it also creates a chaotic close to the class time. To avoid chaos at the end of the period, you should reform the class into a whole group for reporting results of group work, rather than allowing groups to report results from scattered locations in the room. This is especially helpful if chairs or desks have had to be moved to facilitate group work. When the whole group comes together, the classroom is returned to order, all students are facing the correct direction, and the proper attention can be given to each group report.

On Your Own

To develop your own examples of the forced-choice format of structured dilemma, take the following steps:

1. State your current focus of study clearly.

2. Locate or develop a social situation relevant to your current focus of study in which an individual or group must make a decision.

3. Write comprehension and relational discussion starters that you can use to help students read and analyze the social situation.

4. Frame and state three to five possible reactions to this social situation.

5. Make sure the reactions listed are homogeneous.

6. Ascertain that these reactions tend to be good options or bad options so that students are confronted with either choosing the greater good or the lesser evil.

7. Develop an individual decision sheet that cues student behavior and provides a record of personal reactions.

8. Develop a group decision sheet that cues group behavior and provides a record of conclusions agreed to by the members of each group.

THE AFFIRMATIVE FORMAT OF STRUCTURED DILEMMA

Functions

The affirmative format is structured to yield at least five types of student behavior: (1) Each student is confronted with a social situation that requires resolution and is asked to list possible courses of action that might resolve the problem presented. (2) From the list of alternatives developed, each student selects the procedure that is most likely to resolve the social situation given. (3) Each student identifies a criterion that might justify the alternative selected. (4) Students, organized in small groups, share their alternatives and criteria. (5) Each group seeks consensus about what ought to be done and establishes a rationale supporting this position. This group work is then shared with members of other groups.

The affirmative format differs from the forced-choice format in that students are required to develop their own list of options. Whereas the forced-choice format tends to stress that in making decisions, one must often choose the greater good or the lesser evil, the affirmative format emphasizes that actors in a decision-making situation must often initiate their work by developing a range of alternatives.

Description

The affirmative format of structured dilemma contains three components. There is a short story in which an individual or group encounters a problem that demands a decision. There is an individual decision sheet that both cues and structures the reactions of each student. Additionally, there is a group decision sheet that helps members of small groups to share individual reactions as well as seek agreement on both a policy to be adopted and a rationale according to which this decision may be made reasonable to other class members. The groups will need to use their conflict-resolution skills to reach consensus among themselves and with the rest of the class. In other words, the affirmative dilemma is structured so as to secure student behaviors congruent with its function.

Classroom Examples

Five affirmative format examples of structured dilemma are provided here. To enhance your understanding of the components of this format of structured dilemma and of the student behaviors that are likely to be stimulated by this type of decision-making exercise, study at least four of the examples presented. Such understanding will help you consider one approach you may adopt to use this format of structured dilemma.

Trick or Treat

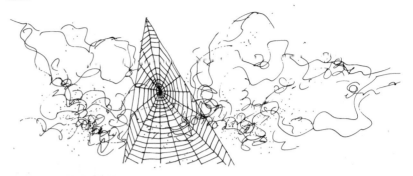

Social Situation

Lydia Spinitz is attending Nob Hill Middle School for the first time. As a new seventh grader, she needs to make friends.

Lydia quickly decides that she would like to be friends with Connie and Juanita. Both are attractive girls who get along well with other students. Both are leaders in all types of activities.

Lydia is happy when Connie invites her to a Halloween party. This will be Lydia's chance to build a good friendship with Connie and Juanita. Lydia promises herself, "I will show them that I can be a good member of their group. I will make them want to be my friend just as much as I want to be their friend."

At first, the party went well. The games were fun; there were many refreshments; and everyone was friendly.

Then Connie and Juanita walked over to Lydia, who was talking with other people. They said, "Come on Lydia. Let's take a walk and get some fresh air."

Once outside, Connie took a cigarette from her purse. Juanita said, "We really like you. We want you to share our cigarette with us. It's our way of welcoming you to the group."

Lydia was very confused. If she smokes, she will do something she believes is wrong. She believes smoking is wrong because it is unhealthy, because she has promised her parents that she will not smoke and because it is a habit that costs a lot of money. For these reasons, Lydia wants to answer with a loud, "No way!"

At the same time, Lydia wants to accept Juanita's offer. She knows that sharing just one cigarette will not hurt her body. She knows that sharing just one cigarette is something her parents are unlikely to discover and will cost her no money. If she refuses, she may never have another chance to become good friends with Juanita and Connie. For these reasons, Lydia very much wants to answer with a loud, "You bet!"

Lydia wants to share the cigarette. Lydia also wants to refuse to share the cigarette. She cannot do both. If she shares the cigarette, she cannot refuse to smoke. If she smokes, she cannot refuse to share the cigarette. These two desires are in conflict with one another. Because these two desires are in conflict, Lydia feels very confused.

Now pretend that you are Lydia Spinitz. As Lydia Spinitz, you want to do the very best thing that you can do in this situation. Use the first decision sheet to guide and record your work.

THE AFFIRMATIVE FORMAT OF STRUCTURED DILEMMA

INDIVIDUAL DECISION SHEET

Complete this decision sheet by yourself. Do not discuss it with other members of the class until you have finished. Later, you will have an opportunity to share your work with other members of a small group.

Pretend that you are Lydia Spinitz. List at least four things that you might do in this situation:

1. _____

2. _____

3. _____

4. _____

The best thing I might do in this situation is to

_____

_____

_____

Suppose someone said your decision was ridiculous. If this happened, how would you defend your choice? My choice is the best one because

_____

_____

_____

GROUP DECISION SHEET

Work with the other members of your group to complete this decision sheet. Later, a member of your group will be asked to share the decisions made by your group with other members of the class.

List the things each member of the group believes Lydia should do in this situation:

1. _____

2. _____

3. _____

4. _____

5. _____

As a group, agree on the single best thing that Lydia can do. You may select one of the recommendations made by a member of your group, or you can find an alternative. We believe the best thing Lydia can do is to

_____

_____

If questioned, we would justify our choice by saying

_____

_____

Group members making this decision are

_____

_____

THE AFFIRMATIVE FORMAT OF STRUCTURED DILEMMA

New Adventures with a New Company

Social Situation

The time is 1617. The place is London, England. Ten shipowners are eating dinner together. They are also talking about their businesses. You are one of these people. In fact, you have been asked to eat with the other nine owners for the first time today.

You are proud to be invited to have dinner with the other ship owners. They are wise people and sharp traders.

In addition, you feel honored. You have worked hard for a long time. You have saved your money and have used your money wisely to make more money. You have earned the right to sit, eat, and exchange trade secrets with these other wealthy people. Exchanging trade secrets with them will help you make more money. The invitation to have dinner with the other shipowners tells you that you have been a successful person.

You are a wealthy man. You own a fleet of seven ships. You have ships that carry cargo from India and the Far East to England. You have ships that sail the west coast of Africa dodging the Portuguese and seeking trade. You have ships that carry goods made in England to Italy, Greece, and the Middle East.

You are proud that you are a rich and powerful man. You want to continue to work and hope to become even richer. In fact, you believe you must continue to work and earn more money. It is a duty that you owe to your God. Since you owe a debt to God, you also owe it to yourself.

You are also a Christian. Although you attend Church of England services, you are really a Puritan. You are called a Puritan because you want to purify the Church of England. You want to make it a church that is really Christian. You are pleased to know that the people with whom you are eating are also Christians and Puritans.

You believe that all men were created by God. Because all men were created by God, you also believe that all men are important. The life of every single person is important.

One of your new friends, Mr. Horn, is talking. Mr. Horn says, "Yesterday, I talked with a man from our colony in Virginia. This man said that Virginia is a rich land. He also said that there are not enough workers to develop the riches of the colony. He said that Englishmen in America would pay good money for servants."

Mr. Horn paused, took a sip a wine, and allowed his words to sink in. He obviously had gained his friends' attention when he talked about good money. Then Mr. Horn continued.

"This started me to thinking. The Spanish buy black men in Africa. They then take these black men to Spanish America where they work as slaves. Sir Francis Drake and Sir John Hawkins made good money buying and selling slaves a few years ago. We, too, might earn a handsome profit in this way.

"We could trade for blacks along the west coast of Africa. We could take the slaves to the American colony. We could exchange the slaves for raw materials and bring the raw materials back to England and sell them. This should give us a good profit. I do not see how we could lose."

A second man, Mr. Winth, interrupted Mr. Horn. "I do not know, Mr. Horn. I have some doubts. None of us has ever traded in slaves before. It is true that we might make good profits. On the other hand, we might lose a great deal of money.

"To do something new is always dangerous. If we were not making good money, it might be worth taking a chance. But we are making good money. I am not sure we should risk the good profits we are making in order to try to increase our earnings.

"I am not sure, Mr. Horn. I am willing to listen further. However, I have my doubts about the new venture."

Mr. Horn answered Mr. Winth. "What you say is true, Mr. Winth. We are making good money. To trade in slaves would be a new adventure for us. To do new things means one must accept risks. Perhaps we should forget the matter for now."

At this point, Mr. Smithe began to speak. "Gentlemen, I find myself agreeing with both of you. I agree with Mr. Horn. To buy slaves in Africa and sell them in America is a way that we can earn good profits. It is our duty to make money, to use what God has given us wisely at all times. I also agree with Mr. Winth. This is a new type of adventure for all of us. None of us wants to run the risk alone. To do so would be foolish.

"What we can do is cooperate. There are ten of us. Each of us can put up one-tenth of the money necessary to send a ship to Africa and then on to the colony in America. If the new trade is profitable, each of us will receive one-tenth of the profits. If the new adventure fails, each of us will only lose a little bit of our wealth.

"All we need to do, gentlemen, is to form a stock company. We could call it the New Adventure Company."

Mr. Horn and Mr. Winth quickly agree. Each man will own one-tenth of the New Adventure Company.

Suddenly, you realize that you will be one of the ten owners of the new company. You will invest your money with them. If the company makes money, a share of the profits will be yours.

At first, you are thrilled. You have always wanted to be part of this kind of group. But you are also upset. You are not sure that it is right to buy and sell men and women. You have heard stories about the voyages of slaves to the New World. You have been told that slaves are mistreated in the New World.

Options

You do not know what you should do. However, you must decide quickly. You can see that the other men intend to join and expect you to cooperate with them.

If you hesitate when you are asked to join, the other men will doubt that you are able to reach decisions quickly. They will doubt that you belong in their company. You will probably never again be invited to have dinner with the other business leaders.

What will you do? Refuse to join the new company? Join? Something else? Use the individual decision sheet that follows to decide what you would do.

INDIVIDUAL DECISION SHEET

Complete this decision sheet before you discuss it with anyone else.

List at least four things you might do in this situation:

1. _____

2. _____

3. _____

4. _____

The best thing I might do in this situation is to

_____

_____

_____

My reasons for believing this is the best thing to do are

_____

_____

_____

GROUP DECISION SHEET

Each member of your group has already made a decision. Now your job as a group is to make one decision that all members of your group believe is best in this situation.

List the choices made by each group member:

1. _____

2. _____

3. _____

4. _____

5. _____

As a group, we believe it is best to

_____

_____

Our reasons for believing our decision is best in this situation are

_____

_____

_____

Group members making this decision are

_____

_____

_____

Good, Better, and Best

Social Situation

Michael and Sam are both good students. They love their English class, and they have always made good grades in that subject.

This year, for the first time, Michael and Sam are members of the same English class. Both have been doing good work in Mr. Johnson's class.

Yesterday, Mr. Johnson returned the first book reports that Michael and Sam had turned in. Each received an A- grade on his book report. They were both disappointed. They were even more disappointed when they found that three other students had received an A grade on their book reports.

On Michael's book report, Mr. Johnson wrote a short note: "Your summary of the book was good. But I wanted to know how you felt about the book. You did not really explain your personal reactions."

Mr. Johnson also wrote a comment on Sam's book report. "I enjoyed reading your reaction to the book. This part was done quite well. Your summary, however, was poorly organized."

After school Michael went to see Mr. Johnson. Michael said, "I have always been the best student in my English class. The other students know I am the best. Why are you trying to ruin my reputation? Just remember, I worked hard for it."

Mr. Johnson tried to explain. "I know you are a good student, Michael. In fact, you are one of my better students. But you did not write an adequate reaction. I want to know how you feel about what you read."

When Mr. Johnson went home, he found a note. The note said, "Please call Mrs. Boykin."

Mrs. Boykin is Sam's mother. Mr. Johnson called her after eating dinner.

Mrs. Boykin said, "I am sorry to interrupt your time at home. However, Sam is very disappointed. I know you would want to know. You see, he had always made the best grades in his English class. He is proud of his record. I would hate to see him become discouraged and begin to do poor work."

Once again, Mr. Johnson explained how he had graded Sam's report. "His summary was not organized well."

At the beginning of English class today, Mr. Johnson asked Michael and Sam to work with three other students. The group assignment was to write a short skit illustrating the meaning of the word *fear*.

Almost at once Michael and Sam became involved in arguments. One of the other members of their group tried to get them to stop. She said, "Listen, you two. We have got a job to do. Let's do it!"

Sam said, "Michael is the problem. I am the best English student in here. He knows it. He just does not want to admit it."

Michael answered Sam at once, "No, you are not the best English student, I am. Before the year is over, I will prove it."

At this point, still another group member said, "Now, you are both wrong. I happen to know that several people made better grades on their book reports than the two of you did. Who are you trying to kid?"

"My goodness," Mr. Johnson thought. "Both of these boys want the other students to think they are the best. This competition for grades is out of hand. I must do something right away."

INDIVIDUAL DECISION SHEET

Pretend that you are Mr. Johnson as you complete this decision sheet. Work alone. Do not discuss your work with others until instructed to do so. List at least three things that you might do in this situation:

1. _____

2. _____

3. _____

As Mr. Johnson, the best thing I might do in this situation is to

_____

_____

_____

The action I recommend is best because

_____

_____

_____

GROUP DECISION SHEET

Work with the other members of your group to complete this decision sheet. Share your individual reactions, decide on one thing that members of your group believe Mr. Johnson should do, and state at least one basis on which you can argue that the decision of your group is best.

List actions recommended by individual members of your group.

1. _____

2. _____

3. _____

4. _____

5. _____

We believe Mr. Johnson should

_____

_____

One basis for believing our decision is best is

_____

_____

Group members making this decision are

_____

_____

A Ship in Trouble

Social Situation

The year is 1786. You are the captain of an American ship with a crew of thirty-five men, carrying a cargo of wheat and hides. Your destination is a port in Egypt. At the present time, you are sailing between Gibraltar and Egypt; your position is almost due north of the city of Tripoli, located on the coast of North Africa.

Pirates from Tripoli are a constant threat to ships like yours. Some countries pay the governor of Tripoli a tribute on a regular schedule. In return for this tribute, the pirates of Tripoli do not interfere with ships that fly the flag of those countries.

Your country is not really a country. You are a citizen of the North American state of Rhode Island, a member of the Confederate States of America. The Confederate States of America is a loose union of states that does not pay tribute to the pirates of Tripoli.

Because your ship might be attacked by pirates, you and your crew are ready to fight. Lookouts are watching the horizon for the approach of other ships. Suddenly, the lookout in the crow's nest cries out, "Ship off the port bow. She's flying no flag."

Using your spyglass, you locate the ship. Apparently the ship is in trouble. Most of its sails are gone, and you can see other signs of damage. It looks as though the ship has been severely damaged in a Mediterranean storm.

A number of men, a few women, and a couple of children are waving shirts and other objects to attract your attention. As far as you can tell, these people are in severe trouble and may die unless you choose to rescue them.

As captain, though, it is your responsibility to protect your crew, cargo, and ship. To meet this responsibility, you have been given the power to command your officers and crew.

You meet with the other officers who help you command the ship and crew.

One officer says, "It is a trick. Let's sail around those tricky pirates."

Your second officer disagrees. "I see no sign that it is a trick. There are women and children on board that ship. Let's sail to their rescue at once."

A third officer suggests a compromise. "Let's take no chances. We can send some men over in a longboat. If it is a trick they will find out. We cannot afford to risk all our men. We must find out whether or not it is a trick. It is better to lose a few men and the longboat than it is to lose our whole crew, cargo, and ship."

THE AFFIRMATIVE FORMAT OF STRUCTURED DILEMMA

The first officer does not like this suggestion. "That is not right. If it is a trick the men we send over are dead men. We should not ask any of our men to take such a chance. We need our full crew to run the ship."

You are the captain. You have the power to make the final decision. You may choose to support one of your officers, or you may decide to do something they have not recommended. You must, however, act, for with the power to command, one must also accept the responsibility to make important decisions.

INDIVIDUAL DECISION SHEET

Pretend you are the captain. List some of the things you might do in this situation:

1. _____

2. _____

3. _____

4. _____

5. _____

The best thing I can do as captain is

_____

_____

If asked to defend my actions, I would use the following arguments:

_____

_____

_____

_____

THE AFFIRMATIVE FORMAT OF STRUCTURED DILEMMA

GROUP DECISION SHEET

List the individual decisions made by each group member:

1. _____

2. _____

3. _____

4. _____

5. _____

We believe that the best course of action for the captain to follow is to

_____

_____

_____

Grounds that we might use to justify our decision are

_____

_____

_____

Group members participating in this decision are

_____

_____

_____

DEALING WITH DILEMMAS

Snack Time, Meal Time, Decision Time

Social Situation

Mrs. Mathers is a kindly lady of eighty-some years. She lives in a neat little house that is just right for her.

Mrs. Mathers is a lady of habit. Her daily routine is always the same.

Each morning she arises at six o'clock. She has a piece of toast, a bowl of oatmeal, a glass of juice, and a cup of coffee for breakfast.

Once the dishes are cleared. Mrs. Mathers sits where she can watch boys and girls pass by on their way to school. She has a friendly wave and a big grin for each boy and girl.

Having rested, Mrs. Mathers cleans her house, takes a bath, and then lies down for a brief nap.

For lunch, Mrs. Mathers has a sandwich, a small bag of baked potato chips, and a large glass of skim milk.

After lunch, Mrs. Mathers makes a batch of cookies. Each afternoon she shares her cookies with boys and girls who stop by to see her. For Mrs. Mathers, this is the high point of the day. She says, "Talking to youngsters does me a world of good. As long as I can talk and be happy with these youngsters, I will remain young."

When the cookie snack is over, Mrs. Mathers again rests for a while.

When she arises, Mrs. Mathers cooks her evening meal. She always has a small salad or bowl of fruit, a serving of lean meat, a vegetable, and a glass of skim milk.

From Monday through Friday, Mrs. Mathers follows this schedule.

On Saturday, Mrs. Mathers's daughter picks her up. They go to the daughter's house for breakfast. Then they go to Mrs. Mathers's doctor to have her blood pressure checked. Mrs. Mathers must do this each week because she is suffering from high blood pressure.

After leaving the doctor's office, Mrs. Mathers goes to the drug store for her medicine for the next week, and then spends the rest of Saturday at her daughter's house, returning home just in time for bed.

On Sunday, she spends the entire day with her younger brother.

This week Mrs. Mathers is faced with a problem. Her blood pressure is up and the doctor has changed her medicine. When she went to the drug store to get her new medicine, it cost twice as much as before.

Mrs. Mathers has a fixed income. She gets a small check each month to pay for the new medicine. In order to pay for the medi-

cine, she would have to change her daily habits.

Mrs. Mathers does not know what to do. She tells her daughter, "I don't see how I can pay for the new medicine. My wants are simple. They have not changed. But now I am no longer able to do the simple things I want to do."

Her daughter replied, "I will help you, mother. Why don't I give you a small allowance each week?"

Mrs. Mathers wanted to cry. She was not a child and she did not want an allowance. She tried to remember that her daughter just wanted to help, but she was angry at her daughter. She wanted to be independent, and this meant she wanted to spend her own money and make her own decisions.

Later, Mrs. Mathers called her brother.

Her brother said, "I will give you a small check each month."

Mrs. Mathers said, "No, thank you!" She slammed the telephone down, angry with her brother.

Mrs. Mathers tried to think of some other answer. She wanted to make a decision that would make her least unhappy.

She said, "I might stop having a snack time for the children. The money I spend on cookies would pay for my new medi-

cine. But snack time is my very favorite time of the day.

"I might stop drinking milk. The price of milk would pay for my new medicine, but I need to drink milk, too."

Mrs. Mathers thought and thought. She was worried and angry. She believed something ought to be done, something that would be fair.

Finally, Mrs. Mathers made the best decision she could possibly make. Imagine you are Mrs. Mathers and complete the decision sheet that follows.

DEALING WITH DILEMMAS

INDIVIDUAL DECISION SHEET

••

As Mrs. Mathers, the things I might do to pay for the medicine are

1. _____

2. _____

3. _____

4. _____

5. _____

As Mrs. Mathers, the best thing I can do is to

_____

_____

I believe this is best because

_____

_____

_____

_____

GROUP DECISION SHEET

Imagine that the members of your group are the children who have cookies each day with Mrs. Mathers as you complete this decision sheet.

List the individual decisions made by each group member.

1. _____

2. _____

3. _____

4. _____

5. _____

We believe Mrs. Mathers should

_____

_____

Our reasons for believing our decision is best are

_____

_____

Group members making this decision are

_____

_____

From the Teacher's Perspective

Initiate the use of the affirmative format of structured dilemma by reviewing the topic, theme, concept, or idea that students are currently studying. Ask students to read the short story that comprises the social situation carefully because they will be expected to respond to individual and group decision sheets based on this situation.

Distribute copies of the social situation and allow students adequate time to read and study the material. As usual, this should be a quiet time free from talk, movement, or other forms of disruptive behavior.

Ascertain that students comprehend the social situation and that they can identify elements of the situation that are related to the topic, theme, concept, or idea of the focus of study. (Conventions according to which comprehension and relational discussion starters may be phrased are found in Chapter 1.)

Distribute the individual decision sheets. Remind students that they are to complete this decision sheet working individually. Stress the desirability of listing as many options as possible that fit the social situation. Walk around the room to determine that students understand the assignment and are following directions.

When students have finished the individual decision sheets, organize them into small groups. Assign students numbers or use some other technique to obtain groups that cut across informal classroom groups and cliques.

Prior to distributing the group decision sheet, define the responsibilities of each group. These are (1) to share individual reactions, (2) to seek a group position, and (3) to articulate a rationale that justifies the position adopted by the group.

Distribute group decision sheets on which each group may record its work. If you wish, each group may select a recorder. Monitor groups to ascertain that all members participate and that their behavior is task-related.

After the small groups have completed the group decision sheets, close the activity. During closure, do at least three things. First, ask one member of each group to share that group's work with other class members. Encourage members of other groups to listen carefully to determine how each group's decision differs from the decision made by their group and to determine how they chose to justify their belief that they have made the best decision. Second, review the current focus of study and highlight aspects of the structured dilemma that are noteworthy in relation to this focus. Third, allow the students to discuss the conflict resolution skills they used in order to reach consensus in their groups. The students may recognize the conflicts within the social situations. The teacher needs to help them recognize the skills of conflict resolution that can be applied to the classroom as well.

On Your Own

To write your own examples of the affirmative format of structured dilemma:

1. Define the theme, topic, concept, or idea that your class is currently studying. (To define is to establish a focus of attention and to establish the significance of this focus.)

2. Find or write a social situation in which a person or group must make a decision. Supply sufficient information for students to assume the role of the person or persons presented in the social situation.

3. Write comprehension discussion starters that you may use to help students understand the social situation.

4. Write relational discussion starters that you may use to help students frame relationships between the social situation and your focus of study.

5. Write an individual decision sheet. The extent to which detailed directions are required depends on the amount of experience your students have had with structured dilemmas. If necessary, refer to examples.

6. Write a group decision sheet. Again, the extent to which detailed directions are necessary is dependent on the previous experiences of your students. If necessary, refer to examples.

THE RANK-ORDER FORMAT OF STRUCTURED DILEMMA

Functions

Suppose that there were two individuals who claimed to hold the following beliefs:

1. It is good to be a faithful member of a large extended family.
2. It is always good to be loyal to one's best friends, no matter the cost of such loyalty.
3. It is good to be truthful and honest in all transactions with other people.
4. It is good to establish, strengthen, and enforce academic standards.

Both of these people may subscribe with integrity to these four beliefs and yet possess belief systems that are divergent. This divergence in belief systems may influence the behavior of the two individuals.

Belief systems may differ significantly and lead to divergent behaviors because the two persons assign different values to the four beliefs to which they are committed. A person who places the highest value on being a good family member may help a relative cheat on a test or be less than truthful if asked by the police to describe the actions of a first cousin. A second person may, with some regret, refuse to help a relative who seeks assistance if such assistance violates the norm of being honest.

Individuals and groups that express commitment to the same norms are likely to subscribe to highly divergent belief systems. Although the same elemental beliefs are used to structure their belief systems, two individuals or two groups may quite easily organize these elemental beliefs differently. The rank-order format stresses the importance of using decision-making skills in groups in order to assign priorities to groups of alternatives.

Description

The rank-order format of structured dilemma contains four components. The first component is a social situation in which an individual
or a group needs to cope with a problem. This social situation
should provide students with sufficient information to allow them to
imagine that they are the persons or the group described in the
social situation. In this respect, the rank-order format does not differ
from the forced-choice or the affirmative format.

The second component is a list of five or more options that are
relevant to the social situation. These may be policies that might be
adopted; a list of consequences that might follow from a decision; or
a list of persons, in conjunction with descriptive data, who are competing for a prize or some other desirable end. The options that
comprise the second component are homogeneous—all are policies,
not a mixture of policies and consequences.

The third and fourth components are decision sheets. Each student
uses the individual decision sheets to rank the options. Small groups
of students use the second decision sheet to seek consensus on the
appropriate ranking of each option. Thus, as is the case with other
structured dilemma formats, individual reactions to a given set of
circumstances can become integral elements of the decision-making
exercise. Whenever disagreements occur, students are instructed to
seek a criterion that enables group members to achieve consensus.
Because of the manner in which the rank-order format is structured,
members of decision-making groups are likely to apply criterial skill
on a number of occasions and on the basis of need. This is to be
contrasted with the forced-choice and affirmative format examples,
which are structured in each instance to require some criterial behavior from students, whereas the rank-order format encourages students
to apply criterial skill because such an application is vital to the completion of the instructional task.

Classroom Examples

Five examples of the rank-order format of structured dilemma are
represented here. Study at least four of them to prepare yourself to
write and use your own examples of this format.

Take Me Out to the Ball Game

CONCEPTUAL FOCUS: CONFLICT

Social Situation

Dustin and Jay are members of the same class. Both enjoy sports. However, they seldom play the same sport at the same time.

Dustin's favorite sport at school is kickball. When the class goes outside for recess, Dustin organizes those who wish to play kickball into two teams.

Jay's favorite sport at school is free-for-all dodgeball. When the class goes outside to play, Jay grabs a ball and starts a game of dodgeball.

This worked well until yesterday, when one of the players kicked the ball too hard. Almost immediately, the ball was flat. This left only one ball for the class to play with.

When it was time to go outside and play today during recess, Dustin tried to grab the one remaining ball for a game of kickball. Jay tried to grab the only ball for dodgeball players.

Dustin grabbed the ball first. Jay knocked the ball out of Dustin's hands. Dustin grabbed it back.

Jay said, "If you do not give me the ball, I am going to hit you. You better let me have it right now."

Dustin answered, "We'll see about that. I had the ball first. Want to fight? Let's go!"

Jay said, "People playing kickball ruined the other ball. This is the ball for playing dodgeball."

Other members of the class surrounded the two boys. Those who wanted to play kickball were on Dustin's side. Those who wanted to play dodgeball were on Jay's side. Others were hoping to see a fight.

Neither Jay nor Dustin could back down now. If Jay let Dustin keep the ball, his friends would say he was afraid. If Dustin gave in to Jay, his friend would say he was chicken.

So Dustin and Jay did what they thought they had to do—they started to fight. Those who supported Dustin cheered for him, and those who supported Jay cheered for him.

The noise attracted Miss Fernandez's attention. She arrived on the run to break up the fight. When the fight stopped, she took the whole class back into the classroom. Then she said, "We cannot have this sort of thing going on. If we are to learn together and play together, we must try to avoid this sort of behavior in the future. I am going to write some things that I might do on the blackboard. Then I will ask you for your help in deciding how we can avoid such disputes in the future."

Options

Miss Fernandez wrote the following statements on the blackboard:

1. I can ask the principal to send Dustin and Jay home for fighting. When their parents come to put them back in school, they will know better than to fight again.

2. I can say that there will be no kickball and no dodgeball until we have saved enough money to buy a second ball.

3. I can say that there will be no more kickball until the group that wants to play kickball has saved enough money to buy a new ball.

4. I can ask the dean to punish Dustin and Jay. They should be taught that it is not good to fight.

5. I can say that no class member will be allowed to play outside tomorrow.

6. I can refuse to let Dustin and Jay play outside for one week.

7. I can ask Dustin and Jay to promise that they will never fight each other or any other person at school.

INDIVIDUAL DECISION SHEET

Complete this decision sheet working alone. Do not discuss it with other members of the class until you have finished it. Later, you will be allowed to share your opinions with some other class members in a small group.

Miss Fernandez can only think of seven things that she might do. Your assignment is to rank these seven things. Write a 1 by the best thing Miss Fernandez might do; write a 2 by the next best thing Miss Fernandez might do. Keep ranking the possible actions until you have placed a 7 by the thing you believe is worst.

_____Send Dustin and Jay home.

_____Ban kickball and dodgeball.

_____Ban kickball, but not dodgeball.

_____Spank Dustin and Jay.

_____Keep the whole class inside tomorrow.

_____Keep Dustin and Jay inside for a week.

_____Ask Dustin and Jay to promise not to fight.

GROUP DECISION SHEET

Work with members of your group to complete this decision sheet. Try to reach an agreement about which is the best solution, and place a 1 by that option. Try to reach agreement about which is the worst option, and place a 7 by that possibility. Then use the numbers 2, 3, 4, 5, and 6 to rank the other options.

_____Send Dustin and Jay home.

_____Ban kickball and dodgeball.

_____Ban kickball, but not dodgeball.

_____Spank Dustin and Jay.

_____Keep the whole class inside tomorrow.

_____Keep Dustin and Jay inside for a week.

_____Ask Dustin and Jay to promise not to fight.

Participating group members are

_____

_____

_____

Up a Neighborhood Tree

Social Situation

For the last four weeks, the Meadows has been a place of great excitement. None of the boys or girls has asked to go to the movies. Television sets have not been used until mothers and fathers turned them on. Children have gone to bed early without arguing with their parents. No boy or girl has been heard to say, "I'm bored, there's nothing to do."

The Meadows is a small housing subdivision. All the houses are built on lots that contain large and beautiful trees.

Across the street, there used to be a forest. For the last year, men have been building a large apartment house there.

Three weeks ago, one of the boys, Brendan, noticed that a lot of old lumber was piled up outside the apartment building. He asked one of the workers, "What are you going to do with this lumber?"

"Burn it," the worker answered.

"May I have it?" Brendan asked.

"And what would you do with it?"

"I would use it to build a treehouse. Then my friends and I could have a club with our own treehouse."

"You may have the lumber," the worker said. "But you must get what you want this afternoon. Tomorrow morning I must burn what is left. Men are coming to sow grass and plant shrubs."

Brendan ran home at once. He went from house to house. He asked his friends to help him get the lumber. He told them that they could help him build a treehouse for their own club.

Soon, twelve boys and girls were moving the lumber to Brendan's backyard. They got more than enough lumber for a treehouse.

The next day, all the children met in Brendan's backyard. They chose a big oak as the place to build the treehouse. They made a list of the tools they would need. Most of the boys owned hammers, and some of the boys' fathers had handsaws they could use. Some of the girls borrowed handsaws and hammers from their parents.

They needed a large ladder. Kaylee's father, who was a painter, had one. When Kaylee asked, he said, "You may use my ladder on weekends and in the late afternoon."

Tools and wood were not enough to build the treehouse. Nails, roll roofing, hinges for a door, and rope to build a ladder from the treehouse to the ground were needed. These things cost money. No boy or girl had enough money to buy nails, roofing material, or a good rope.

Helen made a list of all the things that were needed:

Nails	$ 6.50
Rope	$ 4.50
Roofing	$18.19
Hinges	$ 5.39
Roofing nails	$ 2.60
Paint	$24.50
Total	$61.68

Carlos said, "Wait a minute. When my father painted the garage, he did not use all of the paint he bought. He will let us use it so we won't have to buy paint."

Lisa said, "My dad has a lot of old doors and things. He will give us some old hinges for the door."

Helen removed these items from her list. "Then we still need some $31.79," she said.

All the boys and girls went home and asked their parents for money. When they returned, they all put all their money in an old flowerpot. Helen counted the money. Together all the boys and girls had $32.59. "This is more than enough," she announced.

For almost three weeks the boys and girls worked very hard. Last Friday, the treehouse finally was finished. It had a good roof, safe door, and a great rope ladder. On Saturday morning, Brendan and all the boys met in his backyard, climbed up into the treehouse, and pulled the rope ladder up after them so that no one would bother them.

The boys decided that they would form a club. They called themselves the Meadow Boys. They elected Brendan as their first club president.

They also elected a treasurer, who was told to collect fifty cents in dues each week from every club member. The boys agreed that new boys who moved to the Meadows could join the club but that they must pay an entrance fee of ten dollars.

Later, the girls who had helped build the treehouse arrived. They could not get into the treehouse because the boys had pulled the rope ladder up after them.

Kaylee yelled, "Hey Brendan. Throw the ladder down."

Brendan said, "I am sorry, Kaylee. We have just formed a new club, and it is just for boys."

Lisa demanded, "Give me back my

hinges. Then you can keep your old treehouse."

Helen disagreed. "No! They cannot keep it just for themselves. We helped to build the treehouse. We have got as much right to use it as they have." Brendan's mother and father heard the argument. Brendan's father made all the boys leave the treehouse. Then he said, "I want each of you to ask your parents to meet with me tonight. We will decide how to settle this matter as a group. Until then, no one is to use the treehouse. This includes Brendan."

Options

When the parents arrived, Brendan's father had prepared a list of five things that the parents might do to stop the argument between the boys and girls of the Meadows:

1. We can tell the boys to let the girls who wish to join become members of the new club.

2. We can allow the boys to use the treehouse on Mondays, Wednesdays, and Fridays, and the girls to use the tree house on Tuesdays, Thursdays, and Saturdays.

3. We can ask the boys to think about their decision not to let the girls join, but allow them to make the final decision.

4. We can help the boys build a second treehouse for girls. We can tell them that they may not use their treehouse until one for the girls is finished.

5. We can encourage the girls to build their own treehouse.

INDIVIDUAL DECISION SHEET

Work alone to complete this decision sheet. As you work, imagine that you are a parent of one of the girls who helped build the treehouse.

Rank the list of options prepared by Brendan's father. Place a 1 by the option that you, as a parent of one of the girls, believe is best. Place a 2 by the next best option. Continue to work in this way until you have placed a 5 by the worst option.

_____Force the boys to accept girls as club members.

_____Give the boys and girls assigned days on which they may use the treehouse.

_____Leave the final decision up to the boys.

_____Require the boys to help build a treehouse for the girls.

_____Encourage the girls to build their own treehouse.

GROUP DECISION SHEET

Work with members of your group to complete this decision sheet. Try to reach an agreement about the best thing the parents might do in this situation. Place a 1 by this option. Try to reach agreement about the worst thing the parents might do, and place a 5 by this possibility. Then use the numbers 2, 3, and 4, to rank the other options.

_____Force the boys to accept girls as club members.

_____Give the boys and girls assigned days on which they may use the treehouse.

_____Leave the final decision up to the boys.

_____Require the boys to help build a treehouse for the girls.

_____Encourage the girls to build their own treehouse.

Participating group members are

_____

_____

_____

Buying an Election?

Social Situation

For as long as they can remember, Jane and Sandy have been good friends. Both are seventh graders at Kennedy Middle School.

This year, Jane and Sandy were both nominated to be vice president of the student council. Both were pleased when they were nominated. Both wanted to win. They realized that only one of them would win and the other would lose.

Jane organized her campaign by getting students in her homeroom to help her. They made posters and badges for her and handed out announcements asking students to vote for Jane.

Sandy's parents helped her campaign by giving her money to hire a professional artist to draw posters for her and to have a printer in town print announcements asking students to vote for her. Some members of Sandy's homeroom also helped.

After a short campaign and a school assembly, the students of Kennedy Middle School voted. Sandy was chosen to be vice president. Jane lost by thirteen votes.

After the votes were counted, Dr. Pugh, the principal, told Jane, "You ran a good race. I am proud of you."

Jane answered Dr. Pugh, "I know I lost, but it does not seem fair. Sandy must have spent more than fifty dollars while I spent almost nothing. It is almost like she bought the election."

Dr. Pugh responded, "There is no rule about the use of money in school elections. Since Sandy won without breaking any of the rules, she is to be the new vice president of the student council."

"I guess you are right, Dr. Pugh," Jane sighed. "Well, I will see you around. Thanks."

Later, Dr. Pugh began to think about the election. "It does not seem fair. Sandy may have bought the office. We need some new rules."

Options

Dr. Pugh then listed several things that she might do to avoid the same situation in future elections:

1. I might ask the student council to review election rules at Kennedy Middle.
2. I might appoint a committee of teachers to write new election rules.
3. I might write new election rules and ask the student council to approve them.
4. I might ask a group of parents who are active in politics to write new election rules.
5. I might leave things as they are. This is the first time we have had this problem. It might not occur again.

INDIVIDUAL DECISION SHEET

Pretend that you are the president of the student council at Kennedy Middle School. Dr. Pugh has asked you to rank the five options she has listed. She wants you to place a 1 by the best policy. Place a 2 by the next best policy, etc. Continue to work in this way until you have placed a 5 by the worst option. Do this alone. Later you will be able to share you judgments with those of other members of a small group.

_____Ask student government leaders to review election rules.

_____Ask a group of teachers to write new election rules.

_____As principal, write new election rules, and ask for student council approval.

_____Ask a group of parents to write new rules.

_____Leave things the way they are.

GROUP DECISION SHEET

Work together to complete this decision sheet. As a group agree on the best policy, and place the number 1 by this option. Try to reach agreement about which is the worst policy, and place a 5 by this option. Then use the numbers 2, 3, and 4 to rank the other possibilities.

_____Ask student government leaders to review election rules.

_____Ask a group of teachers to write new election rules.

_____As principal, write new election rules, and ask for student council approval.

_____Ask a group of parents to write new rules.

_____Leave things the way they are.

Participating group members are

_____

_____

_____

The Laws of the Boppers

Social Situation

Once upon a time, there was a country called Bopland. Bopland was not what we would call a civilized country.

Most of the people of Bopland, called Boppers, could not read or write. Very few Boppers could add numbers together; even fewer Boppers could subtract and divide; and no one knew how to work with fractions. Decimal fractions and percentages had not been invented.

Most of the Boppers lived near the only city in Bopland, called Bop Polis. This is another way of saying Bop City.

Bop City owned farmlands, pasture lands, and forest lands around the city. Boppers used the grains grown on the farmlands to make bread. They used the pasture lands to graze cattle, from which they got hides. From the forest, they got wood for cooking, building homes, and making tools.

The ruler of Bop City also received tribute from other cities. Each year, cities sent him gifts of wheat, gold, and other valuable things. These were cities that the rules of Bopland had defeated in wars. If a city refused to pay its tribute, the ruler of Bopland made war against that city.

Because Bop City owned its own farmlands and ruled itself, it was called a city-state. In addition, since Bop City could force other cities to pay tribute, it was also called an empire.

Boppers were ruled by a king. Each year all the people paid taxes to their king. When the king went to war, all adult Boppers could be asked to fight. In return, the king of Bopland defended the cities from others and ruled the city.

As ruler, the king of Bopland made important decisions. He decided what was right and what was wrong. He gave rewards to good Boppers and punished bad Boppers. The people of Bopland said, "The word of our ruler is law." They were right.

Generally, everything worked fine. Sometimes, however, Boppers who did not get rewards from their ruler complained, and those who were punished felt that they had been treated unfairly.

The people who thought they were punished unfairly said, "I did not know that what I was doing was wrong. Had I known, I would have behaved differently."

For a long time, no one did anything about this problem. King after king pretended that the problem did not exist. The people of Bopland tried to pretend that the problem was not present. However, it was hard for Boppers to forget that they might do wrong and be punished, even when they thought they were doing right.

Finally, a ruler of Bopland decided that he would do something about the problem. This ruler was called Boe the Third; he is also known as Boe III to historians.

Options

Boe III commanded a number of Boppers to meet with him. He ordered leading priests, men who knew how to write and carve words on stone, and his most trusted advisors to be present.

When all these persons were gathered, Boe III mounted his throne and began to speak. Some of the important things he said were:

"Boppers, we have a problem. The problem has been with us for a long time. Boppers break the law, and I must decide how they are to be punished. Usually, this works fine. Sometimes, however, those who break the law say that they did not mean to do wrong. They tell me that they did not know that their actions were wrong.

"Many people say they did not know they were doing wrong in order to avoid punishment. These people do not bother me. However, I believe that some of these people are speaking the truth. I do punish people who would not have done wrong if they had known what was wrong."

"When I must punish those who did not know the law, I feel bad. I want to be a fair and good king. I do not want to be remembered as an unjust king.

"I have thought about this problem for a long time. I have discussed it with my priest, with my most trusted advisors, and even with traders who visit our city.

"These people tell me that no ruler has ever solved this problem. Other rulers, like me, are bothered. I, Boe the Third, have decided to solve this problem. I have decided what I will do.

"What we need are some rules that everyone knows. We need to tell everyone what is wrong in Bopland and write down our most important laws. We need to inform all Boppers of the laws and place reminders in important places in Bop City, so that all Boppers may know and obey the law."

"We will begin with five very important laws. These laws are

1. It is wrong to steal. If a man takes property that belongs to someone else, his hands will be cut off so he will not put his hands on the property of another man again.

2. It is wrong to insult our priests, gods, or religion. If a man says a bad thing about a priest, god, or our religion, he will be killed. Those who do not respect our religion will not be allowed to enjoy the good things our gods do for us.

3. It is wrong to kill another man. If a Bopper kills another man, the killer and all members of his family will be beheaded. The killer shall not be allowed to take another man's life. His name will not be carried forward by his children.

4. It is wrong to say bad things about the king. If a man says bad things about the king, his tongue will be removed from his mouth. If a man listens to bad things about the king, his ears will be removed.

5. It is wrong for any man to refuse to be a soldier and fight. If a man refuses to fight, his arms will be removed. Those who are unwilling to use their arms to carry weapons do not need arms."

INDIVIDUAL DECISION SHEET

Working alone, rank order the five new laws of Boe III. To do this, place a 1 by the worst law. Place a 2 by the next to the worst law, etc. Continue to work in this way until you have placed a 5 by the best law. (The law that you select as best may be a bad law. You are only saying that it is better than the other four laws.)

_____It is wrong to steal.

_____It is wrong to insult our priests, gods, or religion.

_____It is wrong to kill another man.

_____It is wrong to say bad things about the king.

_____It is wrong for any man to refuse to be a soldier.

GROUP DECISION SHEET

As members of a group, select the one law that you believe is worst and place the number 1 by this law. Then, select the law that is better than the other four and place a 5 by this law. Then try to agree on the correct ranking for the other laws. When you have finished, you will be able to share your judgments with other members of the class.

_____It is wrong to steal.

_____It is wrong to insult our priests, gods, or religion.

_____It is wrong to kill another man.

_____It is wrong to say bad things about the king.

_____It is wrong for any man to refuse to be a soldier.

Participating group members are

_____

_____

_____

High Hopes, Broken Promises

CONCEPTUAL FOCUS: RELATIVE DEPRIVATION

Social Situation

For the purposes of this exercise, assume that you are a social reformer living in the United States in 1845. Imagine that you know a lot of people like Mr. and Mrs. O'Shea, whom the following story is about. You may also assume that you have the power to try to correct some of the social problems faced by Mr. and Mrs. O'Shea.

In the 1840s, Tom O'Shea and his family left their home in Ireland. They said good-bye to their friends and boarded a ship for America. After a difficult voyage on a crowded ship, they reached the United States.

In Ireland Mr. and Mrs. O'Shea had been poor. They could not provide a good home, schooling, or a good start in life for their children. They heard stories about the United States, a land of opportunity.

"In the United States there are plenty of jobs. If a man has two hands and is willing to work, he is needed."

"In the United States wages are good and getting better. A man can live well and still save money."

"In the United States there are free public schools. Every boy or girl who wants an education can get one."

"In the United States land is cheap. If a family wants a farm, all they need do is work hard for a few years and save their money."

"In the United States men are free. Every man may believe, think, and act as he sees fit."

These stories convinced Mr. and Mrs. O'Shea that they should emigrate to the United States. They expected to build a very good life for themselves and their children.

Mr. and Mrs. O'Shea were disappointed with what they found in the United States. They were forced to live in a crowded apartment house that had only cold running water and two bathrooms for six families.

People in the United States were prejudiced toward members of the Catholic Church, and Mr. and Mrs. O'Shea were Catholics. People in the United States did not like the Irish. Mr. O'Shea was often asked to do jobs, that were considered too dangerous for other workers.

Jobs were not always available. Mr. O'Shea was always one of the last workers to be hired and one of the first to be fired. After all, he was Irish and Catholic.

The schools attended by Mr. and Mrs. O'Shea's children were crowded and were dangerous firetraps. Children of other religious faiths who attended these public schools made fun of the O'Shea children for being Irish and Catholic. The worst teachers were assigned to teach classes that had the most Irish students enrolled.

Mrs. O'Shea had to take a job as a maid to help the family pay rent and buy food. She could not stay home to care for her children.

Mr. O'Shea was not allowed to vote for his own political candidates. Men called political bosses told him who to vote for. If he disobeyed, he might either lose his job or fail to be hired.

Mr. and Mrs. O'Shea became angry. They placed their younger children in a Catholic school so they would not be insulted. They joined other people from Ireland in social groups where they and their family would be treated with respect.

Mr. and Mrs. O'Shea were not happy with their life in the United States. They had wished for a good life they knew they could not have in Ireland. They had moved to America to make it possible for them and their children to live a good life. They came expecting that what they had been told about the United States was true.

In the United States Mr. and Mrs. O'Shea lived far better than they could have lived in Ireland. But they had much less than they had hoped for and expected. They believed that they were deprived of things that were rightfully theirs.

Options

As a social reformer, there are a number of reforms that you might support to help people like the O'Sheas.

1. You could fight against poor housing conditions.
2. You could fight to secure good teachers and good schools for the children of immigrants.
3. You could fight for religious freedom for Catholics.
4. You could fight for improved working conditions for immigrants.
5. You could try to destroy the power of the political bosses.
6. You could fight against bias toward the Irish.

INDIVIDUAL DECISION SHEET

Keep the following in mind: (1) You are a social reformer. (2) You want to help the O'Sheas and others who suffer as they have suffered.

Work alone and rank the six options from best to worst. Use 1 for the best option and 6 for the worst option. When you have finished, you will be expected to share your rankings with other members of a small group.

_____Fight for improved housing.

_____Fight for good teachers and schools.

_____Fight for religious freedom for Catholics.

_____Fight for improved working conditions.

_____Fight to destroy the power of the political bosses.

_____Fight against biased opinions about Irish immigrants.

GROUP DECISION SHEET

Work together to rank order the six policies that social reformers might work for in the situation described in the exercise. Use 1 for the best option and 6 for the worst option.

_____Fight for improved housing.

_____Fight for good teachers and schools.

_____Fight for religious freedom for Catholics.

_____Fight for improved working conditions.

_____Fight to destroy the power of the political bosses.

_____Fight against biased opinions about Irish Immigrants.

Participating group members are

_____

_____

_____

From the Teacher's Perspective

The rank-order format of structured dilemma requires more complex student responses than the standard, forced-choice, and affirmative formats. Hence, it is critically important to establish and maintain a learning set in which students do not lose sight of the focus of the activity.

Learning sets should contain a review of the idea, concept, topic, theme, or issue that students are currently studying; either an explanation or a related discussion about why persons who are committed to the same values or ends may nevertheless possess divergent belief systems; and a general overview of the type of decision-making situation in which students are to work. Do not hesitate to take the time necessary to fulfill these functions thoroughly.

Distribute the social situation and the list of options that establish the constraints within which students are to perform. Stress the need to study the social situation and the options carefully, and maintain a classroom environment free of disruptive behavior.

After students have studied the social situation and options, use comprehension and relational discussion starters to help them understand the social situation (see Chapter 1). By taking this step, you can help students maintain attention to the current focus of study.

When students have demonstrated that they have comprehended the social situation and that they have established its relevance to the current focus of study, distribute copies of the individual decision sheet. When students are working such exercises for the first time, it is necessary to provide careful instructions on how to use numbers to rank objects of valuation. For example, students might need to be reminded that the desired outcome has to play a role in determining which option is number 1. As students gain experience with this type of activity, the need for detailed directions decreases. However, when students are asked to respond to such an exercise without prior experience, detail is important. As students complete the individual decision sheets, monitor behavior to ascertain that they are following directions and are not discussing their individual rankings.

When the individual decision sheets have been completed, explain that the next task is to seek consensus. Remind students that it is important to listen carefully to one another and to learn to disagree without bickering or insulting one another. Students can practice conflict-resolution skills in this manner. Emphasize that where disagreements exist, members of each group should seek some basis other than voting to resolve the dispute. Providing directions such as these between the time students complete the individual decision sheets and the time that they begin to work in small groups increases the odds that the rank-order format will function as intended. The directions must be connected to any classroom conflict resolution policy that has already been established. The connection to existing class structure will enhance the power of both structures.

With clear directions established, divide the students into small groups that cut across informal classroom groups, and distribute the group decision sheets. (Remember the group organizational ideas presented previously.) As students work in groups, observe their behavior to ascertain that members participate and listen; that members make progress toward the completion of the learning task; and that consensus is sought.

To close a rank-order activity, allow one member of each group to share the work of that group with members of other groups. (This can be a volunteer, a role decided during group organization, or a selection by the teacher.) Suggest that students contrast how other groups ranked alternatives with the rankings of their own group. This sharing reinforces the point that values may be organized in different hierarchies, and it provides an opportunity to practice metacognition. It is also advisable to once again review the current focus of study and to highlight some of the ways in which the completed exercise may be related to it.

On Your Own

Use the following steps to develop your own examples of the rank-order format of structured dilemma:

1. In clear language, state the focus of study toward which you wish to direct the dilemma, e.g., topic, idea, theme, or concept.
2. Write a narrative in which one or more persons is confronted with the need to assign priorities to a number of options. Provide sufficient information about the individual or group so that role-taking is possible.
3. List five or more options that can be ranked from best to worst or from worst to best.
4. Develop comprehension and relational discussion starters to help students understand the social situation and relate it to the focus of study.
5. Develop an individual decision sheet. If students have not had previous experience with this type of decision-making exercise, provide clear directions prior to listing the options. You may wish to shorten the options if your class is more experienced.
6. Develop a group decision sheet. For groups that are not experienced with this type of activity, provide explicit directions about the types of student behavior you expect to observe as you monitor the performance of the small groups.

THE CLASSIFICATION FORMAT OF STRUCTURED DILEMMA

Functions

It is not unusual for members of decision-making groups to sort policies they might adopt into three categories. They tend to classify some policies as most worthy or more imperative. They tend to classify other possibilities as being least worthy or less imperative. And they tend to classify a third group of options as being worthy or imperative, but not critically so.

When decision-making groups classify policy options or ends to be pursued, it sometimes becomes important that those policies or ends identified and grouped as most worthy or more imperative are, in fact, most worthy or more imperative. In such situations it is also desirable to offer good reasons for rejecting other policies or ends that are judged to be least worthy or less necessary. Whether groups are focusing on rejected options, preferred options, or both, the task is to generalize items that have been classified according to relative merit and provide criteria that make the assignment of options to categories appear reasonable and fair to others. The classification format is structured to help students acquire and practice skills relevant to this type of decision making.

Description

The classification format of structured dilemma contains at least three components and frequently contains four. These are a social situation, an individual decision sheet to rank a number of options, and one or two group decision sheets that cue and guide groups to classify options into three groups. These groups are most preferred, least preferred, and neither most nor least preferred.

The social situation establishes a condition within which an individual or a group is to make a decision involving at least nine options. Students may be injected into this situation immediately as they are "Cooperation: A Daily Occurrence" and "Three, Three, Three: That's Me and We." "Cooperation" immediately asserts that students in a successful classroom are constantly engaged in acts of cooperation. "Three, Three, Three. . ." begins with the assumption that all of us, rich or poor, suffer at times from relative deprivation.

The social situation may also be developed by presenting a set of social conditions and an individual or group that is attempting to cope with the conditions provided. In this type of social situation, it is important to identify purposes and constraints and to give information about the people who are involved, to enable students to empathize with the persons involved (i.e., to engage in role-taking).

The second component of the classification format is an individual decision sheet that contains either nine or twelve options. Students use this decision sheet to rank the options from the most worthy or imperative to the least worthy or imperative. Except for an increase in the number of options, this component of the classification format does not differ from the rank-order format.

The classification format may contain one or two group-decision sheets. If only one group decision sheet is provided, groups are cued to (1) select the three or four options that are most preferable; (2) select the three or four options that are least desirable; and (3) demonstrate that the preferred options differ from the least-preferred options in a desirable manner.

If two group decision sheets are provided, groups use the first decision sheet to identify the three or four most-preferred options and to identify groups on which it may be argued that those options selected are preferable. This may involve the search for a criterion or the identification of desirable consequences that are expected to result from the selection of these options. Groups use the second group decision sheet to identify the least-preferred options and to identify ground that justify their selection or to analyze possible consequences.

Classroom Examples

Five examples of the classification format of structured dilemma follow. In two cases, the second and fifth examples, students are injected into the social situation almost immediately. In the other three, the social situation is quite similar to this component in other structured dilemma formats. Observe that the decision sheets always list at least nine options and that either one or two Group Decision Sheets may be employed, depending on how you want students to provide justification for the manner in which they chose to classify the given options.

As Others See Us

CONCEPTUAL FOCUS: CONFLICT

Social Situation

Wilson Middle School is located in a large eastern city. When Wilson first opened about five years ago, all of the students enrolled were Anglo Americans.

Even then, there were differences between the students who attended Wilson. Some of Wilson's students came from wealthy families; others came from families that had very little money. Most came from families that were in-between, neither wealthy nor poor.

For the last two years, a new group of students has been attending Wilson. Each year there are more of these students, children of parents who were raised in Latin America.

Recently, teachers have begun to complain about this new group of students:

"These Latin American students all want to sit together. They do not want to make friends with North American students."

"These Latin American students refuse to work on group projects with Anglo-American students. It is almost impossible to get them to cooperate. They are always bickering."

"My Latin American students have chips on their shoulders. They fight with other students at the drop of a hat."

Mr. Ross, the principal, decided to share his problem with an anthropologist at the local university. The professor with whom he talked studies different aspects of Latin American life.

When Mr. Ross explained his problem, the professor said, "Part of your problem is that Latin American students and teachers believe a lot of bad things about Anglo Americans. If you can remove these stereotypes, it will help you solve your problem. There will be less conflict between Anglo-American and Latin American students."

Mr. Ross asked the professor, "What stereotypes about Anglo Americans are held by Latin Americans?"

THE CLASSIFICATION FORMAT OF STRUCTURED DILEMMA **113**

INDIVIDUAL DECISION SHEET

The professor identified nine stereotypes about Anglo Americans that Latin Americans tend to believe. Rank these from the stereotype that would be most harmful to Latin Americans and Anglo-Americans who would like to be friends. Place a 1 by the most harmful stereotype and a 2 by the next most harmful one. Continue to rank the stereotypes until you have placed a 9 by the least harmful stereotype.

_____In North America nearly all the people are violent. The gangster is a hero in North America.

_____In North America nearly all the people want to get rich at the expense of Latin Americans.

_____In North America, most young people take drugs and do other bad things.

_____In North America most people are rich. They like to show off their wealth doing foolish things.

_____In North America, most people are Protestants. They have no respect for the Catholic Church.

_____In North America most people do not use good manners. Wives do not keep the house neat. Table manners are poor.

_____In North America most people are racists. Blacks, Indians, and other minority groups have no chance to succeed.

_____In North America most people support dictators who rule in Latin America. They are in favor of democracy only for themselves.

_____In North America most people have no respect for traditional institutions: the home, the church, and the school.

GROUP DECISION SHEET 1

Work with other members of your group to complete this decision sheet.

The three worst stereotypes are

1. _____

2. _____

3. _____

Why are these the worst stereotypes?

_____

_____

_____

_____

If these three stereotypes were removed, conditions at Wilson Middle would improve in the following ways:

_____

_____

_____

GROUP DECISION SHEET 2

Continue to work as members of a group.

We believe the three least harmful stereotypes are

1. _____

2. _____

3. _____

Imagine that the following conditions were true:
1. All the stereotypes except the three you selected as least harmful have been removed at Wilson.
2. The three you identified as least harmful are still believed by Latin Americans.

If these conditions exist, how might these three stereotypes make it difficult for Anglo-American boys and girls to work with Latin American boys and girls?

_____

_____

_____

Nevertheless, these three stereotypes are the least harmful because

_____

_____

_____

Cooperation: A Daily Occurrence

CONCEPTUAL FOCUS: COOPERATION

Social Situation

The classroom is a social group. Each of us is expected to be a member of this group. Everyone has reason to want the classroom to be a good place in which to study and learn new things.

If the classroom is going to be a good place to study and learn new things, class members must cooperate with one another and with the teacher.

We cooperate when we share ideas and things we own and when two or more of us work together to complete a task.

Nine examples for cooperation in the classroom are listed below. Use the space that is provided after each item to explain why the behavior identified requires cooperation.

1. When we play games, we cooperate. How?

   _____

2. When different class members do different things to build a bulletin board, we cooperate. How?

   _____

3. When we do the work the teacher assigns, we cooperate. How?

   _____

4. When we participate in a class discussion, we cooperate. How?

   _____

5. When we put together a multimedia presentation on the computer, we cooperate. How?

   _____

6. When small groups of students do an experiment in science, we cooperate. How?

   _____

7. When we help break up classmates' fights, we cooperate. How?

   _____

8. When each of us brings something for a class party, such as potato chips, we cooperate. How?

   _____

9. When we plan and do a group project, we cooperate. How?

   _____

INDIVIDUAL DECISION SHEET

Complete this decision sheet working alone. Nine ways in which members of a class may cooperate are listed below. All nine can be important. Some are probably more important to you than others. Your task is to rank these from the one that is most important to the one that is least important.

_____Playing games

_____Building bulletin boards

_____Completing assigned work

_____Speaking and listening during class discussions

_____Working on a computer presentation

_____Conducting science experiments

_____Helping enemies become friends

_____Sharing cookies and other good things for a party

_____Planning and doing a group project for class

GROUP DECISION SHEET 1

As a group, we believe that the three most important ways members of our class can and should cooperate are

1. _____

_____

2. _____

_____

3. _____

_____

If all members of our class cooperated in these ways, the class would be better in the following ways:

_____

_____

_____

_____

GROUP DECISION SHEET 2

The three least important ways in which we might cooperate are

1. _____

   _____

2. _____

   _____

3. _____

   _____

Suppose members of your class never cooperated in these three ways. How might this make your class a bad place in which to study?

_____

_____

_____

_____

These three are least important because

_____

_____

The Science Project

CONCEPTUAL FOCUS: COMPETITION

Social Situation

Webster Middle School contains four grades: fifth, sixth, seventh, and eighth. Webster Middle School is just five years old.

For the last four years, the science teachers at Webster Middle School have sponsored a science fair. Boys and girls are encouraged to complete science projects. These projects are all displayed in the school cafeteria.

When the science teachers started the fair, they hoped for two results. First, they hoped that the science fair would make the study of science more exciting for students. Second, they hoped that parents would attend the fair and become better informed about the science program at Webster Middle School.

The science teachers have been disappointed. Few students have completed science projects to display at the fair. Most of the student projects that have been displayed have been poorly done. Very few parents and almost no students have attended the fair.

This fall, the science teachers met to discuss the fair. One teacher said, "The science fair is not working. We should cancel it. It is a lot of work for us, and we are not getting results. It is just not worth keeping."

A second teacher said, "I disagree. What we need to do is require student projects. We must require each student to complete a project that is worth displaying."

A third teacher joined in. "No, we should not cancel the fair. Having the fair is still a good idea. We have to build up the interest of our students.

"Requiring projects is a poor idea. We want students to enter the fair because they are interested, not because they are forced to do so.

"What we need is a contest. We should award prizes for each grade. When students realize that they can win prizes, they will get busy."

The first teacher answered, "I like that idea. The prizes ought to make the idea of a fair work. If students are competing, they will be more interested."

The second teacher added, "Their parents will be more interested as well."

The teachers listed nine possible prizes:

1. A chemistry set
2. Trophies
3. A visit to a museum of natural history
4. Equipment for collecting rocks
5. A weekend of camping and nature study
6. A microscope
7. A nature study kit
8. A computer
9. A CD player

At this point, one of the teachers said, "I do not think we should decide what prizes to offer until we find out how our students would react to these types of prizes."

The other teachers agreed. They, too, thought it would be good to get the opinions of some of the students who attend Webster Middle School.

INDIVIDUAL DECISION SHEET

Complete this decision sheet before you discuss it with anyone else. Rank the prizes from the best to the worst. Place a 1 by the prize that you believe would be most likely to encourage students to enter the science fair. Place a 2 by the next most effective prize. Keep doing this until you have placed a 9 by the least-effective prize that might be offered.

_____A chemistry set

_____Trophies

_____A visit to a museum of natural history

_____Equipment for collecting rocks

_____A weekend of camping and nature study

_____A microscope

_____A nature study kit

_____A computer

_____A CD player

GROUP DECISION SHEET

Imagine that you are a committee of students that must recommend prizes to the science teachers. Remember, the purpose of the prizes is to get students more interested in the science fair.

We believe that the three best prizes are

1. _____

2. _____

3. _____

We believe that the three worst prizes are

1. _____

2. _____

3. _____

Some reasons the best prizes are better than the worst prizes are

_____

_____

_____

Susan's Plight, Dora's Power

CONCEPTUAL FOCUS: POWER

Social Situation

Imagine that you are a twelve-year-old girl name Susan. You live in Eagle Town, a town of 30,000 people. You and Dora have been best friends for many years.

Dora lives across the street from you. For more that two years, she has delivered the *Clarion*, the local newspaper. Dora has used the money she made delivering the *Clarion* to buy a new bicycle, new clothes, and once, to visit Disney World with a group from her church.

While Dora was out of town, you were her substitute. You delivered her papers, and she always paid you $5.00 for each day. For Sunday, she always paid you $7.50 because Sunday papers are heavier.

You have always been ready and willing to deliver Dora's papers for her. You have been glad to earn the money, and you admire Dora and like to do things to help her. Most importantly, Dora has promised to recommend you as the person to replace her when she quits. She has always promised that she will help you get the paper route.

Three weeks ago, Dora decided that she would deliver the *Clarion* for six more weeks and then quit. She called her boss, the district manager, and recommended that he select you to replace her.

The district manager met with you, your parents, and Dora. He explained the job. He explained how much money you would make each month and how you would pay your bill, and best of all, how you could earn bonus money.

"For each week that you deliver the *Clarion* and no customer complains, you earn an extra dollar of bonus money. If you deliver the paper for an entire month without a complaint, you earn six dollars in bonus money."

Finally, the district manager said, "Susan, the job is yours if Dora tells me you know the route and can do the job when she quits. Between now and the time that Dora quits, you can practice the route and learn how to keep clear records."

At first you were happy to help Dora roll the papers, and place them in plastic bags. You were pleased to carry the papers and deliver them to the houses as Dora taught you where customers live. You knew Dora was training you so you would be able to do a good job.

For the last week though, you have not been happy with Dora. You have rolled almost all the papers and delivered all of them. In fact, you are doing all Dora's work for her, but she is the person who will be paid.

You do not think this is fair. At first, you thought you would just do the work. After all, the route and the money will be yours next month. Lately, though, you have begun to wonder what you might do. You have even made a list of things that you might do. The list of things that you might do is presented on the first decision sheet.

THE CLASSIFICATION FORMAT OF STRUCTURED DILEMMA

125

INDIVIDUAL DECISION SHEET

Working alone, rank order the things that you, as Susan, might do in this social situation. Place a 1 by the most preferable option and continue until you have placed a 9 by the least preferred option.

_____I might save some of my schoolwork and do it at home. This means that I can tell Dora I would love to help her with the papers but I am too far behind in my schoolwork.

_____I might ask my mother to tell Dora that I must help her with housework. This means I will be in the house helping my mother and cannot help Dora with the papers.

_____I might tell Dora I have learned all I need to know and will not help her again unless she agrees to pay me. This means I will tell Dora she cannot continue to treat me unfairly.

_____I can continue to do Dora's work for her, but I can tell her she is being unfair. This means that I will let Dora know that she is not fooling me.

_____I can tell Dora's parents what she is doing. This means that I hope they will make Dora treat me fairly.

_____I can call the district manager and report Dora. This means that I hope the district manager will force Dora to treat me fairly.

_____I can tell Dora's other friends how Dora is behaving. This means that I hope they will shame her into treating me fairly.

_____I can continue doing Dora's work but make a few careless mistakes. This means that customers will complain and Dora will lose bonus money.

_____I can tell my parents what is happening. This means that I hope they will do something to protect me from Dora.

GROUP DECISION SHEET

You and other members of your group are to imagine that you are good friends of Susan and Dora. You are to agree on the three best and three worst things that Susan might do.

The three best things Susan might do are

1. _____

2. _____

3. _____

The three worst things Susan might do are

1. _____

2. _____

3. _____

Important and good ways in which the best things differ from the worst things Susan might do are

_____

_____

_____

Three, Three, Three: That's Me and We

Social Situation

People who are deprived want something they believe to be good and something they believe they should be able to have. For some reason, they do not have the ability to obtain the thing they want.

Imagine that you might be deprived in nine different situations. Later, you and members of a small group will select the three situations in which you would most prefer to be deprived, if you had to be deprived. You are also to select three situations you would most prefer to avoid, if you could avoid some situations.

To complete this exercise, do three things in the following order:

1. Read each situation carefully, and then tell why it is a condition of relative deprivation. Use the comprehension guide to record your answer. Tell why you would feel deprived if you were the person in each story.
2. Rank the stories. Place a 1 in front of the situation you believe would be the worst to find yourself in. Place a 2 in front of the situation you believe would be next worst. Continue doing this until you have placed a 9 by the best of the nine situations. Use the Individual Decision Sheet.
3. Work with your group in order to complete the two Group Decision Sheets.

SITUATION A
Abraham has been making a grade of C in his science class. He wants to make good grades. This grading period, Abraham worked harder to make good grades. When he started working harder, a grade of 80 percent was required for a B. This grading period, Abraham had an average of 84 percent in science.

The teacher said, "Only students who had an average of 85 percent earned a B for this grading period."

SITUATION B
Mike has two brothers and two sisters. With his parents, they all live in a three-bedroom house. Mike's parents use one bedroom, his sisters use a second bedroom, and Mike and his two brothers use the third bedroom. They are quite crowded.

Last month, Mike's father started building a new bedroom. Mike and his brothers were very excited. They told their friends.

"Now we will have more room for our books and toys, and we will be able to ask our friends to spend the night with us."

Last night, Mike's father and mother told him a secret. She said, "I am going to have a baby. Dad is building a new nursery where the baby will sleep."

SITUATION C
Ralph and his father bought five acres of land in the woods. They saved their money so they could buy lumber and build their very own cabin.

Ralph's sister goes to a local college. Last week, the college decided to charge more money.

Ralph's father said, "We have no choice. We will use the money we had saved to build a cabin and sell it to pay the college tuition."

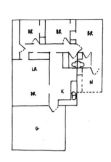

SITUATION D

All the children at Belcher Elementary School were quite excited because the school board was building a new library for their school.

The old library was so small and crowded that each class could visit it only once every two weeks. There was no room to read magazines, watch videos, or listen to tapes or CDs.

The new library was to be almost twice as big as the old one. There would be room for reading magazines, watching videos, and listening to tapes and CDs. Each class would be able to go to the library often.

Last night, the school board decided that more students should attend Belcher Elementary School. More than twice as many students as are now in the school will be going to Belcher Elementary next year.

Jennifer cried when her parents told her what had happened.

SITUATION E

Nancy lived near a small stream and wanted to fish in it just like the boys and girls she watched.

Nancy did not know how to fish. Since her father did not live with her mother, he could not teach Nancy.

Nancy's mother said, "I'll tell you what. Spend a month of your summer vacation with your aunt, who will teach you how to fish."

Nancy spent most of the next summer with her aunt. When she returned home, she knew how to fish.

Her mother told her, "Nancy, there is a new factory upstream. The fish in the river aren't edible."

SITUATION F

Steve wanted to get a job delivering papers. He went to the office of a man at the newspaper.

The man at the newspaper said, "You are only ten years old. All our carriers must be eleven years old."

The next year Steve went back to see the man at the newspaper. The man said, "Let's see, you are only eleven. We now insist that all our carriers be at least thirteen years old."

SITUATION G

Last year, all the girls in Sharon's school started wearing torn jeans to school.

Sharon told her mother, "I want to have a pair of jeans like the other girls have. They are 'in.'"

Sharon's mother said, "We cannot afford to buy you new jeans just because they are in style. I'll tell you what I will do. Your older sister will soon outgrow her jeans. When she is too big for them, they will be yours."

Sharon said, "I suppose I will have to wait."

This year Sharon wears a pair of jeans to school once a week. All the other girls are wearing shorts and blouses to school.

Sharon tells her mother, "I do not want to wear jeans to school. I need to wear shorts and blouses."

Sharon's mother said, "That's just too bad.

You wanted jeans, now you have a pair. I just don't know what it takes to make you happy."

SITUATION H

Claire is one of the best athletes at Watson Junior High School. All the boys and girls want her to be on their team. She is a good hitter, throws a softball farther than any of the students, and runs faster than anyone else.

But Claire is disappointed. When there is a school dance, none of boys asks her to dance. The boys who want her to play on their teams try to avoid her at school dances.

Last year, Claire noticed that the boys really liked cheerleaders. All the boys wanted to dance with cheerleaders.

Claire practiced and went out for cheerleading. She was elected and is now a cheerleader. Still, all the boys want her to be on their softball team. None of the boys invited her to dance at the last school dance. She is still a pal and not attractive to the boys.

SITUATION I

Johnny and his father are great sports fans. Each winter they go to the mountains and ski, and each summer they go to Florida for deep-sea fishing.

This year they decide to learn to water-ski. Johnny's father bought a speedboat and water skis, and they both took lessons.

Just when they were ready to start having fun, Johnny's father was asked to go to Central America and work. He told Johnny, "We will have to forget waterskiing for two or three years. How would you like to learn mountain climbing?"

DEALING WITH DILEMMAS

COMPREHENSION GUIDE

Situation A is an example of relative deprivation because

_____

_____

_____

Situation B is an example of relative deprivation because

_____

_____

_____

Situation C is an example of relative deprivation because

_____

_____

_____

Situation D is an example of relative deprivation because

_____

_____

_____

THE CLASSIFICATION FORMAT OF STRUCTURED DILEMMA   **131**

Situation E is an example of relative deprivation because

_____

_____

_____

Situation F is an example of relative deprivation because

_____

_____

_____

Situation G is an example of relative deprivation because

_____

_____

_____

Situation H is an example of relative deprivation because

_____

_____

_____

Situation I is an example of relative deprivation because

_____

_____

_____

INDIVIDUAL DECISION SHEET

Rank the conditions of relative deprivation. Mark the story showing the worst deprivation with a 1; mark the story that is next worst with a 2. Keep doing this until you have marked the situation that is most preferable with a 9. Do this individually.

_____Abraham

_____Mike

_____Ralph

_____Jennifer

_____Nancy

_____Steve

_____Sharon

_____Claire

_____Johnny

GROUP DECISION SHEET 1

Imagine that you and your group must suffer from relative deprivation as three of the boys and girls in the stories did. Select the
three conditions you would choose to experience.

If we had to suffer from relative deprivation, the three situations
we would accept in order to avoid the other six are

1. _____

2. _____

3. _____

What bad effects would you fear if you found yourself in these
three situations? List as many bad effects as members of your
group can identify.

1. _____

2. _____

3. _____

4. _____

5. _____

GROUP DECISION SHEET TWO

Suppose you and other members of your group could avoid only three of the conditions of relative deprivation. Which three would you avoid?

1. _____

2. _____

3. _____

Assume you could not avoid these conditions. What bad things might you do because you were suffering from relative deprivation? List as many bad things as members of your group can identify.

1. _____

2. _____

3. _____

4. _____

5. _____

From the Teacher's Perspective

Classification structured dilemmas may be used much like forced-choice, affirmative, and rank-order structured dilemmas are used. Some of the common teacher tasks are

1. To provide a lesson set that reviews the topic, theme, concept, idea, or issue that is at the focus of study.

2. To distribute the social situation and maintain a period of quiet time in which students may comprehend the social situation and search for aspects that are relevant to the focus of study.

3. To use comprehension and relational discussion starters to enhance student understanding of the social situation and to help students frame relationships between the situation and the focus of study.

4. To secure individual reactions to the rank-order decision sheet so that students may carry personal beliefs into their group work.

5. To use randomization or some other procedure to organize small groups that differ from the informal social groups already present in the class.

6. To monitor the performance of group members in order to intervene, if necessary, and in order not to interfere if the group requires no assistance.

7. To allow each group to report its findings and how these conclusions were reached to the total class. (The students who are listening should contrast how they worked in their groups with how the reporting group reasoned.)

8. To provide lesson closure that highlights significant ways in which the structured dilemma is related to the current focus of study.

The Group Decision Sheets are, of course, different from those used in other dilemma formats. When students are just beginning to work with group decision sheets for the classification format, you need to explain very carefully that all members of a small group need not agree on the relative priority of the preferred options. If, for example, student A ranks an option as being the most preferable and student B ranks the same options as being the third best, the two are in agreement that the option is to be classified as one of the best. Again, when students are just beginning to work with this format, it is usually easier for them to respond to two group decision sheets than it is to one. If two group decision sheets are used, students should first concentrate on the best options and then on the worst options. In contrast, when only one group decision sheet is provided, students must deal concurrently with best and worst options. This is a more difficult task.

DEALING WITH DILEMMAS

On Your Own

By following a few directions and referring to examples of the classification format presented in this chapter, you may write your own examples of this type of structured dilemma. To write your own examples:

1. Clearly state the topic, theme, concept, or issue that your students will be studying when you use the structured dilemma.

2. Develop a social situation relevant to the focus of study.

3. Within the social situation, present a person or a group that is coping with a social problem.

4. Write comprehension and relational discussion starters for the social situation. (In two of the examples, a comprehension guide was included as part of the social situation.)

5. Develop at least nine options that provide those persons present in the social situation with alternatives. (You may use twelve. If you do, students classify four as best and four as preferable.)

6. Use the nine options to develop an individual rank-order decision sheet.

7. Write a group decision sheet that focuses student attention on the best options.

8. Write a group decision sheet that focuses student attention on the worst or least-preferred options.

ONCE OVER VERY LIGHTLY

Helping students with an opportunity to develop and apply decision-making skills that are applicable in structured dilemmas are important goals of instruction in the middle grades. This responsibility does not belong to any single area of study; rather, it is shared by teachers in such different bodies of subject matter such as science, social studies, English, foreign language, and reading.

Structured dilemmas written in five formats can help students develop and apply their skills as members of decision-making groups. Structured dilemmas in five formats can also help students develop and practice conflict-resolution skills that can then be applied to other situations. The five formats are the standard, forced-choice, affirmative, rank-order, and classification structured dilemmas.

The *standard* format adds a personalization dimension to the comprehension and analytical skills typically used to understand and use information found in standard instructional resources.

The *forced-choice* format provides students with practice in choosing the greater good at the price of other good things or in accepting the lesser evil in order to avoid greater evils.

The *affirmative* format stresses that decision-making groups frequently begin to function by developing a range of alternatives. This range of alternatives then defines the universe from which a decision is to be derived. The universe of a group will develop individually and differ somewhat from the original universe of alternatives.

The *rank-order* format highlights how people who hold the same beliefs may organize these beliefs into divergent systems. People from different social or cultural groups may find themselves in conflict because of the divergent manner in which they organize beliefs that are quite similar.

The *classification* format, as its name implies, emphasizes that decision-making groups often classify objects of value into three classes: those that are most worthy or imperative; those that are worthy or imperative; and those that are least worthy or imperative.

To write and use a standard format of structured dilemma, develop three types of discussion starters. These are comprehension, relational, and value/feeling questions and directions. While using other formats of structured dilemma, use comprehension and relational discussion starters to ascertain that students are ready to respond to decision sheets. When groups are sharing how they have reacted to group decision sheets, use value/feeling questions to challenge, clarify, or extend what is reported to the total class. Conventions may be used in order to structure and phrase comprehension, relational, and value/feeling questions as described in Chapter 1.

Decision-making behavior and the associated valuing behavior—in response to forced-choice, affirmative, rank-order, and classification structured dilemmas—is cued and guided by two decision sheets. The first decision sheet is completed by students working individually. The second decision sheet is completed by a small group of students. Divergent reactions to the first decision sheet trigger students' efforts to intersuade and to find a consensus.

Small decision-making groups should contain a good mix of students. Random assignment of students tends to yield groups that differ from the informal social groups that exist in the classroom. Some methods for assigning students to groups are discussed in Chapter 2.

Classroom teachers with subject-matter responsibilities may and should write and use structured dilemmas that are directly relevant to the content they are teaching. Their use is likely to increase student comprehension and retention of information. To do this, teachers may refer to the examples and conventions presented at the end of each chapter.

For example, students in an American history class discussing the civil rights movement can use materials based on the events at Little Rock Central High School in 1957. In order to develop social situations, teachers could use *Warriors Don't Cry*, by Melba Pattillo Beals. This book provides numerous situations from which any format of structured dilemma could be created. Students could demonstrate their understanding of the material using the standard format. They could be forced to choose from the greater good or the lesser evil, as the soldiers of the National Guard and 101st Airborne Division were forced to do, using the forced-choice format. They could develop alternatives to situations and decisions, such as identifying the worst things the students had to overcome and the best things they enjoyed, through the affirmative format. They could see how individuals react to situations differently, through the comparison of individual students' reactions to the social situation, using rank-order dilemmas. And they could establish criteria with which they can categorize the actions of those involved in the social situation using the classification format. The possibilities are as endless as the materials available.

DEALING WITH DILEMMAS

A number of teaching skills are relevant to the use of structured dilemmas: establishing learning set and providing closure; structuring directions and questions that will help students comprehend and relate to the social situation on which the dilemmas are based; providing clear directions as students move from one form of activity to another, especially to individual and group decision sheets; monitoring individual and group behavior, intervening as necessary to help students to work effectively; and providing avenues for metacognition for students to recognize how and why they made the decisions they did. Although dilemmas are structured to require and allow individuals and groups to work independently, you, the teacher, remain the important and influential agent of learning.